We Feed Each Other:
Nourishment through Friendship

A Memoir of Sorts

Ellen J. Dehouske

In Honor of My Mother

Dedication:

In her 30s, Eileen sailing her Hobie Cat, a small
sailing catamaran, in Biscayne Bay, Miami, Florida

This book is dedicated to my sister, Eileen, who has been, from earliest childhood, the epitome of what a friend is. It is dedicated to her and to my many other sisters and a few brothers, who have made this journey in life meaningful, loving, caring, and rich. Thank you.

Table of Contents

Wine and Cheese

Soup

Salad

Dessert

Apéritif

Acknowledgments

I would like to thank my friend, Elizabeth-Anne Kim, who has encouraged me as a writer and guided me through the self-publishing process. She also provided ongoing editing and commenting that proved vital. My appreciation goes to Karen VanderVen for her additional proofreading. My life story writing group, facilitated by the caring Sharon Lippincott, gave ongoing encouragement and feedback about the essays and stories. Olawale Williams in collaboration with Kary Arimoto-Mercer united my theme of nourishing one another through food and friendship with a visual representation for the cover. The title emerged after suggestions from my dear friend and author, Dee Giffin Flaherty, and my Osher Life Long Learning instructor at the University of Pittsburgh, Pam O'Brien. My dear friends, Martha Ezzell, Sandie Turner, and Dee Giffin Flaherty listened to me read many of my stories and essays during our retreats over the last fifteen plus years together and provided ongoing suggestions and encouragement. To all of these folks, I say a huge thank you.

Preface

The roots of relationships and recipes are intertwined with my family and my life. They whetted my appetite for life as one who not only survived but ultimately thrived.

Because of the tie between food and friendship in my life, I have titled this memoir of sorts based on a Jewish allegory in which a person must choose between heaven and hell. The guide shows him hell with a sumptuous table set with food and utensils so long that the miserable people starve because they cannot put the spoons and forks in their mouths. The guide then shows the person heaven where he sees the same sumptuous table and long utensils surrounded by happy people. The person asks the guide why the people in heaven are happy, and the guide responds, "These people feed each other." In my life, too, I find that my friends and I feed each other in many ways.

Growing up, my sister, Eileen, and I were orphans of a sort. We were like mashed potatoes and gravy that had somehow gotten separated from the rest of the entrée. My mother was absent all of my life by way of her 13-year psychiatric hospitalization, and I don't remember my father, who died in a car accident when I was two. I loved my life with my grandfather, who let me eat all the creamed corn and mashed potatoes that I wanted. Unfortunately, he died of a heart attack when I was seven. I had food wars with Aunt Mary and Uncle George but otherwise had a rather happy home for the first few years of my stay with them until I was 12 when she was hospitalized on a psychiatric unit. Aunt Julia cooked all of my favorite foods in my teen years but was very strict, rigid, and mean, so they were unhappy times. Yes, we were "kept in the family" as the nuns from the orphanage encouraged of the family, but I never felt that my sister and I belonged anywhere really except with Grandpa.

But, through it all, Eileen and I stuck together.

The only constant was my sister who remained with me growing up but moved quite a distance away to Florida as an adult. Since I never had one family to belong to as a child and did not marry at a young age, I have created a family of long-lasting friends in my adult life, and they have agreed to this arrangement. These friends are my family.

I participated in a life story writing group and formulated the idea of a book of writings about my life—stories and essays about my friends—and collecting favorite recipes from them to accompany these written pieces. The themes of friendship and food were integrated—as adults, we nurtured and nourished each other. A memoir with my friends' recipes was what I wanted to produce.

Format

The format of this book is straight-forward. Each section of the book is about one group of my friends. The community established in each group is a powerful demonstration of caring. Often, but not always, each member of the group relates to the other members of the group to form a whole. Each person presented in this book is someone who has profoundly impacted my life through relationship. I tell a story or write an essay about that person and her/his relationship to me. Here, I include a photograph of the person so that some of their personal karma will be part of the book. I also wanted you to meet each friend as I introduced you to her/him. Then I present a favorite recipe that that person has chosen to include in the book.

COCKTAIL HOUR

Enjoying a glass of wine to stimulate the palate before
the dinner begins

With a New Eye

Me at three-years-old

While I was reading the book titled *Wild: Lost and Found on the Pacific Crest Trail* by Cheryl Strayed, I looked at the back of the library book jacket and began to read the various reactions to the book by other authors. One immediately stood out to me, *Motherless Daughters: A Legacy of Loss* by Hope Edelman. The phrase "motherless daughters" from the title intrigued me. It dawned on me.

I was a motherless daughter.

The idea had never occurred to me before because I had a mother, who was alive during my childhood, adolescence, and adulthood. But she was on a psychiatric unit for my first 13 years of life, and I rarely saw her. When I did see her, she did not interact with me. Even after she was released from the hospital and I saw her on rare occasions at family functions, she did not connect with me. She was physically and emotionally non-existent in my life.

In her book, Hope Edelman emphasizes that, after the mother leaves, a motherless daughter requires that not only her physical needs but also her emotional needs be met. She also needs a release of feelings. When a child loses a mother, she needs opportunities to express her sadness in a secure environment that will allow her to integrate her loss and avoid serious ongoing distress. I was not afforded that opportunity.

My family cared for me in other ways. Grandpa playfully rode me on his wheel chair and lovingly made me cinnamon toast and milked-down coffee for breakfast when I was four. Aunt Mary made Campbell's tomato soup for lunch, and Uncle George gave me a nickel for a bag of Snyder's potato chips to eat on the street car ride to school. But no one talked to me about Grandpa's death and Aunt Mary and Uncle George's giving me up to Aunt Julia and Uncle Joe. I was not encouraged to talk about my feelings about anything, let alone my mother's absence.

I grew up feeling ashamed of my mother because she had a mental illness and because she was absent. It was worse to have an emotionally unavailable mother who was absent than it would have been to have a mother who was dead. Hope Edelman states that a dead mother is "honorable" (p 83) while an absent mother leaves a sense of "degradation and unworthiness" (p. 83) in the daughter. In fact, when people asked—which rarely happened—I said my mother was dead, killed in a car accident with my father, who died in a car accident when I was two.

As a young person, I never really mourned the loss of my mother. Again Hope Edelman asserts that, without going through the grief of mother loss, the daughter has a "veneer of strength" (p. 11) but hasn't dealt with the emotions at the core. I talk about the absence of a mother in a most perfunctory way—without passion and emotion. I have a generalized fear of loss and abandonment. Yet I appear strong. I haven't cried about the loss of my mother, but I have cried about a gazillion other things. I cry easily. I cry at sad movies. I cry at happy movies. I cry sometimes when someone gives me a gift. I tear up with tender comments and stories. It seems that tears are always close at hand.

Perhaps the most dramatic time I cried was when I was collecting data for my research on my doctoral dissertation. I had designed a workbook to help teachers facilitate story-writing with emotionally troubled adolescents and respond empathetically to the characters in the stories. A little paranoid, I feared that some teen who was writing stories would commit suicide and I would be blamed because I had encouraged the teen to get in touch with difficult feelings symbolically through writing stories. I had forgotten Fred Rogers' mantra: if it's mentionable, it's manageable.

I cried all over town at restaurants as I was discussing my fears. I cried in my soup; I cried in my salads. Tears fell on my grilled chicken sandwich. I cried everywhere as I was eating lunches and dinners with my friends. I had put myself in a maternal role with these teens, but I did not know how to be a good mother—I never had one. I couldn't keep them psychologically safe because I was never kept safe.

With my first job after getting my PhD, I worked for a psychiatrist who had previously been a terrific consultant at the adolescent psychiatric unit where I worked. In this new position, he was to be my supervisor, but did not do his job. He was burnt out and unavailable to me. I was working in a school district where several of the students had been reported to have been, in years passed, abused at home. I could not help them feel safe—again, how could I be the good mother when I had never had one? I didn't know what it was like to be a good mother.

I was so beaten down by the dissertation process that I didn't know how to ask for help or to keep myself psychologically safe. I was falling apart. I kept slugging it out, trying to do a job which I was not able to do. Most people would have quit and not blamed themselves for the failure. I did not quit and blamed myself for the situation. I ended up hospitalized on a psychiatric unit. Being hospitalized was emotionally charged. I was ashamed of myself for letting it happen to me after all I had done to avoid it. I had read. I had studied. I had gone to therapy. It *still* happened to me. I feared that, like my mother, I too would spend 13 years in a psychiatric unit.

I did have a veneer of strength for most of my adult life. I called it a strong exterior with a hollow core. I didn't know why. I saw it most clearly when I was hospitalized. I could not call upon a strong inner power to keep myself safe. Again, how could I? I had had no mother to teach it to me. My mental illness took the shape of weakness, vulnerability, confusion, fear, and exposure. But this hospitalization was a transition from being "one tough cookie" to showing her soft inner self. The confrontation with my own mental illness was also an internalization of my own mother. Finally I was no longer pretending that she was not my mother.

This transition from being tough to being softer began during the dissertation process. I had always been a stellar student and had prided myself on it. During the dissertation process, however, I was just one of many stellar students. To complicate the situation, I had brain freeze during the oral defense of my overview and dissertation. I do not do well when confronted. I knew my research well but did not answer confidently and thoroughly. I passed but felt inadequate. I did not show what I knew. This uncomfortable experience began stripping away my veneer of strength, letting me begin to discover my softness and let it show through.

By contrast, reading Hope Edelman's discussion of the motherless woman's success interested me, and I found myself identifying with multiple aspects of it. I am autonomous and have a sense of personal power. I am quite independent in my thoughts and actions but less vocal than I once was about my own opinions. I was proud of being a part of 5% of the women in this country who held a PhD when I earned mine. And I have always been mature beyond my years and have taken responsibility for my own life, for example, by living over 40 years on my own and caring for myself. I've made a good life for myself in spite of all I've been through, and I am proud of that.

Motherless daughters have creative outlets for self-expression, and that resonated with me. Creative self-expression allows these women ways to examine themes of abandonment and such. Water color painting, crafts like candle making, creative writing, journaling, cooking, and innovative teaching are some aspects of creativity that I have indulged in over the years. These can be opportunities for me to work through the grief of being a motherless daughter like I am doing now. However, since I never had a mother present, it's hard to mourn the mother I never had. These creative endeavors are also ways to use self-expression to nourish my spirit and develop my maternal traits.

My mother as a young woman

Likewise, I always felt unique and isolated because I had a mother with a mental illness, who was hospitalized long term. I always felt different from others. I *was* different from others. I was an orphan of sorts, who had no real mother. That put me at a distance from my peers. I did realize this, but to me it was because my mother had a mental illness. I did not recognize that feeling unique and isolated was also a result of having an absent mother. This uniqueness and isolation have diminished as I have arrived at an age where most of my friends are motherless daughters and orphans too.

Indeed, I do have resilience and determination. One way I showed this fortitude was when I fought the university where I was hired to keep my job after my fourth hospitalization on a psychiatric unit. It occurred in October of my first year teaching at the university. The university put a lot of pressure on me to leave. However, I felt I had a right to my job, and the law was on my side. The Provost and the Dean kept meeting with me to try and dissuade me from returning. I enlisted the support of a state senator's mental health advocate and contacted a lawyer who worked pro bono, the Labor Relations Board, and the United Mental Health Alliance. Finally I threatened to go to the newspapers with the story. The university relented. I remained there, and, at the beginning, my career was a great struggle. I felt self-conscious about the faculty's knowing that I had been hospitalized, but I slogged through, doing my job. Over my time there, I became highly regarded as a tenured faculty and leader. I retired Professor Emerita to a standing ovation from the faculty after 22 years of service. I'm proud of that.

Hope Edelman asserts that one way motherless daughters distinguish themselves is through creating meaning. Although I have a good sense of humor, I am not frivolous; I am serious-minded. From a young age, I embraced the gravity of life. I am insightful and reflective. I enjoy the challenge of trying to figure things out—to make meaning out of life's experiences. In fact, from time to time, my friends Janet, Sandie, and Martha try and tone down my seriousness!

This cookbook of friends which includes a page describing the special way that I relate to each friend—friends who became the family I never had—and a special recipe which each has selected to include in the book, is one of the ways I am creating meaning. It is my attempt to concretely nourish myself and others—a theme I've dealt with all of my life. It is a lifelong theme of a motherless daughter who was not nurtured and nourished by her mother and had to learn how to do it herself and through her friends. Furthermore, a community of friends is established over the food. This is one positive resolution to being a motherless daughter.

So, as I examine my life using the new lens of being a motherless daughter, I have found that I have experienced a lot because of the motherless daughter status. It has resulted in my being fiercely independent, resilient, strong (perhaps even tough at times), highly responsible, and creative. Being a motherless daughter has come to make me who I am today. It has not condemned me to a life of strife and struggle nor held me back from success, but I carry her loss with me in everything I do and experience.

HORS
D'ŒUVRES

Relationships and recipes rooted in my family. They whetted my appetite for life as one who not only survived but ultimately thrived.

Family

Childhood

Family means a lot to me because I never really had one. I use the term family broadly. My sister Eileen is a year younger and the only constant family I really had as a child. In actuality, Grandpa and various aunts and uncles took us in to live with them from time to time, but we didn't really belong with anyone. We went in and out of several relatives' homes throughout childhood and adolescence, but we always remained together.

Food was always important in every house I lived. No matter what, having good food to eat, and plenty of it, signified comfort, success, and being taken care of. Whatever the budget, food was a top priority. Every night, we had home cooked meals like breaded chicken, mashed potatoes, and corn. On Sundays chicken and beef vegetable soup and pot roast graced the table. Breaded pork chops were a well-loved favorite too. The wonderful aromas filled each house all day long as the cooking proceeded. Yes, no matter what the dish, food was used to nourish and nurture the body and the soul in my family.

Holidays signified veritable feasts. Traditional celebrations included turkey and all of the trimmings like stuffing, gravy, mashed potatoes, sweet potatoes, cranberry sauce, vegetables, and rolls. Alternate holidays had ham and the accoutrements. They were the typical, all-American holidays. Also, ours was a large family of five aunts and two uncles, mostly all married and with children, so when we all got together for at least part of the holiday, these were joyful, festive occasions for a child. This is all part of the backdrop of my childhood and adolescence, which also held untold sadness. On one hand, I felt at home, and on the other, I felt like a visitor.

My mother came and went in my life, but I never really knew her. She was hospitalized on a state psychiatric unit for the first 13 years of my life. Even after that I rarely saw her. She was probably just trying to keep herself together and stay out of the hospital. Remarkably, she was able to live on her own and take care of herself. She is the saddest person that I have ever known personally. Yet she was very skilled in the kitchen as a single, young woman, working as a cook for a doctor and his family. I have included a recipe from her family of origin, **Hungarian Stuffed Peppers**, as her recipe.

Grandpa was the first caretaker I remember when our mother was placed on a psychiatric unit and our father was killed in a car accident. He was a loving and caring man, who nurtured us in his house until he died when I was seven. He bought a house where our mother, father, my sister, and I, and all of the single aunts and uncles could live. When my mother was hospitalized and my father was killed in a car accident, Grandpa kept us in his house and lovingly watched over us. He also was the cook, and some of the wonderful aromas of that time still linger in my memory. His **Chicken and Beef Vegetable Soup** was still his children's favorite meal, and they made it the way he did.

Then we moved in with **Aunt Mary and Uncle George**. We lived happily with them for several years until Aunt Mary had a child and experienced a deep post-partum psychosis. In the early 1950s, there was no adequate diagnosis and treatment for this disorder. Eileen and I remained with Aunt Mary and Uncle George, who tried to nurture me through my eating issues. School lunches often were wonderful **Grilled Cheese Sandwiches and Tomato Soup**. From them I have my **Hearty Pot Roast** recipe for Sunday dinner.

During this time and afterward, **Aunt Molly and Uncle Leonard** played a vital role in our childhood and adolescence. Their home was a place where we could come to have fun. We especially enjoyed playing with **Cousin David**. We visited their house and took pleasure in doing what regular kids did in their free time. We played croquet, went swimming and had picnics. During all of these wonderful, fun-filled visits, I also remember Aunt Molly's delicious **Cheese Cake**.

I rarely saw **Aunt Goldie and Uncle Ernie** because they lived in East Cleveland, on the other side of town from most of the family. However, every holiday, they joined the family gatherings. They were always kind to me. Aunt Goldie's **Chicken Paprikash with Dumplings** is included.

Eileen and I spent a lot of time together playing as children. We were never abused; we were unintentionally neglected. Left to our own designs, we creatively approached every day as a new opportunity for adventure. We played by ourselves or with neighborhood friends, but we always played, often inventing our own activities. We created a play idea where we **Roasted Hot Dogs** as a part of it.

Adulthood

As adults, **Eileen** and I continue to remain emotionally close although we live far apart. She lives in Gainesville, Florida, and I live in Pittsburgh, Pennsylvania. We still have grown up adventures together. We also have become excellent cooks. Eileen's **Stuffed Cabbage** is a culinary delight.

Eileen adopted two sisters, Lee-Ann and Anita, who are adults now. Eileen moved to West Lafayette, Indiana, for 5 years to continue to room with her roommate and friend while she was completing a PhD. At this time, the children were young and then pre-adolescents, and I had a family to visit and share all holidays with—it was only an eight-hour drive away. I got to know Lee-Ann and Anita much better because I saw them more frequently.

Lee-Ann's Five Bean Chili reminds me of our camping trips.

Anita's Sweet Potato Casserole is wonderful comfort food.

Over the last ten years, **Aunt Margie**, who was only ten years older than me, became a consultant in my cooking. She would share the strategies of the Eberlings about beef and chicken vegetable soup, egg dumplings, cabbage and noodles, and more. We talked on the phone frequently and shared ideas. I would tell her about making cold sweet pea and basil soup, and she would explain creating her own meatloaf recipe. We also discussed cooking tips in general. Aunt Margie loved to bake. Her famous **Coconut Bars** were treasured by all the family and a favorite dessert for her to bring to all family functions.

I include my best friend, **Janet**, in the section called family because she is family to me. We have been friends for five decades, and she is my other sister. She has been a wonderful, loyal friend over the years. I have spent many a visit to her home for dinners and particularly for the holidays. We have spent many times together dining out in restaurants and talking. She can always be counted on to help me think through a problem for she is very supportive and kind. Janet is also a wonderful cook as I can attest to from spending many of those holidays and dinners with her family. Likewise Janet has a terrific sense of humor and is just plain fun to be with. Janet's Puerto Rican heritage presented itself in the side dish, **Red Beans and Rice**, and, the main dish, **Arroz Con Pollo**.

Included are two recipes of my own in this section of the cookbook. In my twenties, I showed an interest in cooking, but it was soon displaced by a career. I became a perfunctory cook, who just did the bare essentials to get the job done. Now, in retirement, I have renewed my interest in cooking. I have included **Pecan Pie** from my youth and **Home Style Skillet Chicken** from my retirement.

Under the Dinner Table—Note on a Green Envelope: My Mother

My mother and father on their wedding day with Aunt Molly, Aunt Julia and Aunt Goldie in the wedding party

Having a house means a lot to me.

As I have grown older, it has often worried me that, although I've worked hard all of my life, I've never earned a lot of money. I suppose I was afraid that I would be one of those people who did not have enough retirement money to pay rent, buy food, and afford medicine. Although for many years I didn't have a house, I now have one.

Having a home means even more.

When I was a child, I never had a permanent home. My mother was hospitalized shortly after my birth in 1945 and spent the next 13 years on a state psychiatric unit after undiagnosed post-partum depression/psychosis. Such things were not well understood in those days. My sister and I were cared for by a variety of my mother's family members. I never was allowed to deal with the feelings of loss. No one ever talked about them.

When my mother was discharged from the hospital in 1958, she moved in as a boarder in someone's house and was employed as wait staff at May Company's best restaurant, where she worked for over 25 years. During this time, she would visit from one relative to another.

My sister and I always felt great compassion for our mother. My mother did not relate to Eileen and me. She was not unkind; she was just non-existent as a mother. I don't remember calling her "Mother" or hearing her refer to us as her children. And I was totally disconnected from those sad feelings. I accepted that reality. No one ever talked about that.

My relatives did not talk much about my mother. There was a lot of secrecy in my family. Part of it is due to the fear and stigma of mental illness. Many years later, I was to talk with Aunt Goldie, an in-law, who was willing to discuss painful family experiences. I asked her why no one ever helped my mother when she first came out of the hospital. Aunt Goldie told me that the doctor advised my family not to let my mother live with any of them—to let her be independent.

My mother wore no make-up and fixed her hair in a loose bun in the back of her head. She was a sturdily built woman who donned clean, simple skirts and cardigan sweaters. During the years she worked, my mother saved money diligently in order to buy a house—her dream. In a relatively short time, because of her relentless saving, she did purchase a small, new row house in the city of Cleveland. She paid cash. I really don't know if she felt proud of herself. I hope she did.

As the years progressed, I heard very little about my mother—and never asked about her. I practiced the silence of fear. I wondered if she ever liked me. I saw her infrequently—maybe once every five years. During this time, my sister and I graduated from high school and went our separate ways to nursing school and to college. I guess we needed to grow and develop separately—and we did. I worked as a high school English teacher, special educator, and college professor. Eileen was a pediatric nurse and then a nurse educator. We were both very proud of making something of our lives—of overcoming great barriers.

In 1988, when I began teaching in the early childhood education program at Carlow University, I also began writing to my mother, sending note cards monthly. I wanted to provide her with the opportunity to get to know my sister and me and to communicate with me if she wanted to do so. I placed my name and return address on the envelopes so that she would recognize who was writing and could choose to not open the notes if that was what she wanted. Also, I feared that she might have been rejecting me all of those years and would not want to hear from me.

Those notes were my effort to let her know that my sister and I were okay. They were also an attempt to connect with her if she wished to connect with me. I fantasized that I would pick her up and bring her to Pittsburgh and my friends would warmly receive her. But I never spoke about this to anyone.

My mother died in May of 1993. Her death was a very sad day because I knew with finality that I would never come to know her. However, I was soon to discover some very important information about her because my sister and I were called upon to plan her funeral. We wanted to give her as typical a funeral as we could. We had an obituary in the newspaper. We also had a mass, a eulogy by a priest, a cemetery service, and a stone marker.

We learned some things about my mother's recent life. Her job for the last ten years was as a cook at the Federal Building cafeteria in downtown Cleveland. She came in to work on Mondays hungry, so her employer suspected that she did not eat much on the weekends. Her house was sparsely furnished but clean. A neighbor found her over a pail of soapy water scrubbing the living room floor. My mother was 77-years-old when she died of heart failure. She was wearing an apron and in its pocket was the last note card that I had sent her—opened. At least, she got to know a little bit about Eileen and me.

My sister and I did not want to clear out her house. It seemed too tragic to bear. My uncle Bernie and my cousin Bernie agreed to do it. They found a small box with all of the opened note cards that I had sent. They also discovered a pale, mint green business envelope on which she had written lightly in pencil. These were her words just as she wrote them:

> *Dear Ellen and Eileen,*
>
> *How are you both. I miss both of you. I want you to come home and the 3 of us will go out and buy a house. I have all of the money. I am fine, a bit tired and I'll wait for you.*
>
> *Love to you both.*
>
> *Mother*
>
> *September, 1991*
>
> *I love you both dear.*

I had the note framed and displayed it in my living room. I wanted to give the note and my mother a home with me.

Uncle Bernie and Cousin Bernie also discovered taped to the underside of the kitchen table a plastic bag with a bank passbook for a savings account inside. The amount in the account was $150,037.09. Amazingly, she had saved this amount of money and had saved it for my sister and me. This was especially poignant since her last few W-2 forms showed that she had earned between $6,000.00 and $7,000.00 a year as her income. She had saved nearly everything.

I knew that I would use my half to purchase a small house. A year later, I found my townhouse. It was perfect for me, and I felt good when I was in it. It fronted Copeland Street in Shadyside, a fashionable, urban, residential area. The living room, at the rear of the house, was one of my favorite spaces. It had lots of natural light from floor-length windows. The rattan furniture inside was upholstered in shades of rose and green. Thrown over the couch was an afghan I had crocheted 25 years earlier. It matched the colors of the couch perfectly. The best part of the living room was the log-burning fireplace. I had always wanted one. The fireplace created an atmosphere of comfort and calm for work, contemplation, relaxation, and companionship. I used it every day that I could.

The fireplace in the condominium that I purchased with the money my mother left me. I loved using it for myself daily and with friends whenever the occasion arose.

For many years, I liked heavy wooden furniture. In the years prior to buying this house, I had found myself drawn to the light and airy nature of rattan and wicker. It paralleled the transformation that I had gone through personally. The items in my house, although acquired at different times, fit together in color, style, and a feeling of comfort. It seemed as if I knew what this house would be like—as if I had been preparing for this house my whole middle life.

When I was walking around the house sometimes or reading a book, I would feel the presence of my mother in my home. I felt well cared for. When I played Puccini in my home, I remembered how she loved opera music, and I thought that she would have liked this house. This is the home that my mother gave me, the very best home that she could. I was very grateful and thankful for it.

She had thought about me.

But it's a bittersweet story because I never really knew my mother, and she never knew me. We both practiced the silence of the fear of rejection. We never took a chance. No one encouraged me, and I never encouraged myself. That's how powerful fear is.

But we did think about each other.

Hungarian Stuffed Peppers: Toltott Paprika

When my mother was single, she and two other single sisters, worked for a doctor and his family who were Hungarian. She was the cook and created many Hungarian dishes in the fashion of her mother, my maternal grandmother. This is one of her main courses for a dinner of the family of the doctor.

Ingredients:
4 green bell peppers
1 small onion, finely chopped
1 lb. ground chuck
½ lb. ground pork
½ c. uncooked rice, rinsed
1 large egg, beaten
1 t. salt
1 t. sweet or hot Hungarian paprika
½ t. black pepper
1 clove garlic, finely chopped
2 (8-ounce) cans of tomato sauce
1 t sugar
sour cream for garnish (optional)

Directions:
Wash peppers. Cut off tops and remove seeds. Season cavities lightly with salt and pepper.

Finely chop pepper tops and place in large bowl.

Add onion, ground chuck, pork, rice, egg, paprika, salt, pepper, and garlic in bowl with pepper tops and mix well.

Stuff peppers lightly with meat mixture because rice will expand. If you have any leftover meat filling, form it into meatballs.

Place peppers and any meatballs in a Dutch oven. Mix together tomato sauce and sugar and pour over peppers.

Cook in a 350 oven or on the stove top for 1 hour.

Serve peppers with a dollop of sour cream, if desired, and crusty white or rye bread. Cooked peppers freeze well if covered with sauce.

Yield: 4 stuffed peppers.

Comfy Foods: Grandpa

Grandpa at a family picnic with Uncle Ernie and some youngsters

Grandpa at a family picnic drinking a beverage

Grandpa had a kind face and a bald head. These are things a young child notices.

He had muscular arms because he rode around the first floor of a very big, three-story, old stone house in a manual wheel chair. He had no legs because he had lost them to diabetes. He wore trousers with long pant legs folded up over at the knees and pinned shut with large safety pins. A young child notices this too. Grandpa would ride Eileen and me around the house on the foot rest of the wheel chair—we would take turns standing on it, hanging on to the arm rest and shrieking with delight.

My memories go back to three- or four-years-old with Grandpa. Every national holiday morning, Grandpa hung the flag, and we sat on our large, stone front porch to watch the parade move past our house and into the cemetery opposite us. The veterans in the parade would then give a 21-gun salute to end the ceremony. Our family was moved to witness these parades and the salute. Grandpa, Eileen, and I and any other visiting family members shared in this annual event.

We also had a small stone back porch, and Grandpa would wheel to the door in order to scooch off of the wheelchair, scooch across the small porch, bump his butt down the stairs, scooch to a platform he made of a chair seat and roller skates, and go out into the back yard—specifically, to his backyard garden. He would put on some gloves to keep his hands clean—and also to protect them from cuts. He would roll along a path to his garden and tend to it to provide the family with delicious fresh tomatoes, lettuce, cucumbers, green onions, and green peppers. Although I never knew my grandmother—she died right after I was born—it is said that her wonderful, warm baked bread and Grandpa's fresh vegetables made quite a delicious sandwich, although Grandpa always let me have all the creamed corn and mashed potatoes that I wanted. Grandpa and Grandma were nurturers. Eileen and I were fortunate.

Inside the house, I remember that, in one room on the first floor, Grandpa had a bed and a table beside it with a glass of water on it where he kept his false teeth at night. Again, something a young child would notice. Grandpa said that, if he had known false teeth would feel so good, he would have gotten them years ago.

There was a huge kitchen. Grandpa was always in the kitchen cooking. He was quite a fine cook. But what I remember the most is that, every morning after Aunt Margie went to high school and Aunt Julia and Uncle Billy went to work, Grandpa, Eileen, and I had a morning ritual. I was about four-years-old, and Eileen was three. Grandpa would give us each a huge cup of coffee with a lot of milk and sugar. He would burn toast in the grill of the oven and scrape the burnt part off. I never knew whether his burning the toast was accidental because the grill malfunctioned or intentional because he thought it tasted better. I was curious but never even asked about it. He then buttered the toast, put cinnamon and sugar on it, and gave us each a piece. I gobbled it down, always feeling well-loved and well cared for.

In those days, children were to be seen and not heard. Also, family business was not only not discussed outside of the house, but in our family, it wasn't even talked about inside of the home—not even burnt toast.

I learned to be more questioning and vocal as a young adult, but my Grandpa died when I was only seven-years-old, so I never did find out why the toast was burnt—or a lot of other things that were important and not so important. It seems sad to me today that my family never talked about things—I was such a talkative child. I could have enjoyed what I have valued in my adult life—the pleasure of talking through the problems of life. How could I rejoice in my family's overcoming obstacles if no one would admit there were any? Now, I have a sister and good friends who provide for this. I enjoy the conversation.

No life is perfect, and, truly, nothing can take away from the feelings of care that I received from my Grandpa who nurtured me when I was a young and vulnerable little child. I loved him dearly and am very grateful for his six years of loving care in my early life. He gave me the foundations for feeling valued and cherished.

Epilogue: By the way, it was years later, as a middle-aged person, that I discovered a huge white cup at a garage sale. I knew I had to have it, but I had no idea why. It took months for the memory to surface. It was like the cups we used at Grandpa's morning ritual.

Grandpa showed his tenderness and care for us by cooking nearly all of the meals for the house. Eileen and I had a favorite of his, Chicken and Beef Vegetable Soup. The first ingredient was his great love for us. Here is the rest of the recipe for it.

Chicken and Beef Vegetable Soup

Ingredients:

2 chicken breasts, with bones
1 beef shank, skinned
Vegetable group 1 (use fresh whole vegetables unless
    otherwise noted):
    6 carrots
    1 large onion
    3-4 small tomatoes
    6-8 cloves garlic
    celery, sliced in half and tied together
    cabbage
    parsley roots, with leaves tied together
    1 small green pepper
Vegetable group 2:
    1 potato
    1 small cauliflower, with greens removed and cut
    into 4-5 pieces
1 12-oz. bag noodles, any type desired
salt and pepper to taste

Directions:

In a pot of cold water put 2 chicken breasts with bones
and skin and a beef shank. Boil and skim the residue
from the top with a hand strainer.

Add vegetable group 1.

1½ hours later, add vegetable group 2.

Add salt and pepper to taste.

Cook at gentle simmer for about 2 hours

Strain through a colander. Place broth in one container. Place vegetables in another container.

Cook noodles in a separate pot as directed on package and place them in a separate container.

When reheating soup, take the needed amount of broth, chicken (deboned, without the skin and cut in pieces) and pieces of beef, vegetables and noodles and place in a pot.

Note: Also interestingly, once when I talked to Aunt Molly when she was in assisted living, and asked her, "What food do you miss most?" She replied, "Chicken and Beef Vegetable soup." When I asked her to tell me how she made it, it was exactly like this.

Aunt Mary and Uncle George

Aunt Mary was a gentle woman. She and Uncle George cared for Eileen and me beginning when I was seven-years-old—after Grandpa died.

Aunt Mary had honey blond, long wavy hair, cut in the fashion of the early fifties. She was tall, had a slim figure and wore attractive clothes. Aunt Mary and Uncle George wanted a child but couldn't have one so they took us in. They cared for us well.

Every Saturday night, after Eileen and I would bathe, Aunt Mary would roll our hair in curlers to get us ready for Sunday church. Afterwards, there would be a lot of talking and giggling as she tucked us in bed. We each had our own twin bed in one bedroom.

Sunday mornings, we went to church dressed in lovely dresses and shiny patent leather shoes with white ankle socks—and we had curly hair. We returned home to a breakfast of doughnuts and milk—Uncle George always brought home fresh doughnuts on Sunday mornings so we had this treat when we arrived from church.

We had an ordinary life. During the week, not only did Aunt Mary stay home and care for the house and cook dinners every evening, but she also prepared our lunches—we came home from school every day. We often had a bowl of Campbell's tomato soup and a sandwich—our favorites. Uncle George, who worked second shift and was home for lunch, gave us the fare for the trolley ride back and forth to school and a nickel each for a bag of Snyder's potato chips on our return to school.

We also played a lot with the neighbor children in the front yard. The back yard was full of trees; we climbed there. We enjoyed school-aged children's games like jump rope, hopscotch, and football. I became a Girl Scout and loved collecting badges.

For my first, Holy Communion, which is a very big event in the Catholic Church, I had a party. The family was all invited. I even had an ice cream cake—my favorite. I wore a beautiful white, lace dress with a lace veil for the ceremony. I also received many presents—there were five aunts and two uncles in my mother's family. What a festive occasion.

I was delighted to be dressed so beautifully on this special day of my first Holy Communion.

Uncle George was an important ingredient in this mix. He was a kind and gentle man, tall, thin, and handsome with brown, wavy hair. He worked for Standard Oil in Ohio as a laborer, a hard-working man and a fine role model for a strong work ethic. Also, once, while Uncle George was working second shift, three to eleven, he called home to tell Aunt Mary to take us into the basement with a flashlight and the battery-operated radio for a tornado was approaching. He always cared for us.

When I was young, I was a very picky eater. Until he died, Grandpa let me eat all the mashed potatoes and creamed corn that I wanted. I was especially sensitive to textures and smells and could gag at the simplest provocation with foods that put me off. I was very thin.

When I moved in with Aunt Mary and Uncle George, things changed around food. Uncle George believed I should eat what was on my plate or sit at the table and then go to bed. He was worried about me because the school weighed me one year and I was 52 pounds, and, the next year, I still weighed 52 pounds. Probably out of frustration and anxiety, he called upon me to eat everything on my plate, even noodles and cabbage.

Finally, to my relief, an enlightened doctor told Uncle George to let me be, and I'd eat when I was ready. He did, and I did. I was grateful to that wise doctor—and I'm sure Uncle George was grateful as well for he could relax, and our power and control issues over food were settled.

One year, Eileen and I planned a little birthday party for Uncle George. We went into the basement—where we hid everything—put on lovely dresses and brought up a cake and Dad's Old Fashioned root beer to surprise him. He was surprised.

Eileen and I had found another nurturing environment to live in—we were very fortunate.

After living with them for about three years, Aunt Mary got pregnant—as often happens. Everyone was delighted. Debbie was born and was an easy baby. But Aunt Mary got sick. People didn't know much about post-partum depression and post-partum psychosis in those days. So our little household struggled on by ourselves.

Eileen and I began to play outside of the house and in the woods and at the creek—unsupervised. It's amazing that safer times and luck resulted in nothing bad ever happening to us. We also cared for Debbie as much as we could—and brought her outside to play in the yard often. Uncle George tried to care for us all, but things began to breakdown. Uncle George was slow to act, so we lived in this limbo for several years. Finally, under the pressure of the family, he placed Aunt Mary on a state psychiatric ward for what would be six months. Psychiatric care was undeveloped in the 1950s, especially at state hospitals.

Eileen and I would have to move again. This time—one day away from an orphanage and with two newly purchased suitcases—Aunt Julia and her new husband, Uncle Joe, agreed to take us in.

Grilled Cheese Sandwiches and Tomato Soup

Ingredients:
4 slices white bread
4 t butter, solid
2 slices American cheese
1 10¾-oz. can Campbell's tomato soup

Directions:
Butter one side of each slice of bread with 1 t butter.

Place slice of American cheese in between the unbuttered parts of the bread.

Fry each sandwich in the frying pan on low medium heat until each side is golden brown

Simultaneously cook the tomato soup according to the recipe on the can.

Hearty Pot Roast

I have included this recipe for Aunt Mary because, when she was well, she made delicious meals for our family. This was a favorite.

Ingredients:
3-pound beef chuck roast
2 T oil
3 c. water
8 small potatoes, peeled and halved
8 medium carrots, halved crosswise and lengthwise
8 small onions, halved
salt and pepper to taste

Directions:
Heat oil in a Dutch oven. Brown meat over medium heat, about 15 minutes.

Reduce heat, add water, simmer on top of range or bake in oven for 4 hours at 325 degrees until meat is tender. Do not open pot while cooking.

About 1 hour before end of cooking time, add vegetables.

Make gravy using the directions below.

Serve with meat and vegetables on a platter.

Gravy
Ingredients:
Drippings from the roast
2 T cornstarch, mixed with a small portion of water
  until pourable

Directions:
Pour drippings (fat and juices) from the Dutch oven
into a bowl, leaving brown particles in the pan.

Let fat rise to top of drippings. Skim off fat.

Cook over high heat, adding corn starch mixture
gradually, stirring until the gravy is smooth and bubbly.

Remove from heat.

Delicious:
Aunt Molly and Uncle Leonard

Aunt Molly and Uncle Leonard at the wedding of their son Dave to Janis

When I told Aunt Molly that I was writing my memoirs, she said, "Okay, but no bitterness or sadness." While I don't believe in glossing over pain, I didn't have any problem with Aunt Molly's dictate in this case. Summers were fun with Aunt Molly and Uncle Leonard. I visited frequently between the ages eight and 12. I anticipated the fun of our visits. I especially remember the ongoing joyfulness, laughter, and pleasure. Also, Aunt Molly and Uncle Leonard were nurturers—Aunt Molly nourished through food, and Uncle Leonard nourished through activity.

For several years, my sister, Eileen, and I spent our Friday evenings with Aunt Molly, Uncle Leonard, and my cousin David, who was three years younger than me. They picked us up from Aunt Mary and Uncle George's on Fridays after work at about 5 o'clock. We drove to Smith Quarry to swim. Eileen was seven, I was eight, and David was five. We enjoyed splashing around in the chilly water, beginning the steps to swim—holding our breath, kicking, and floating. Uncle Leonard was teaching us.

Me, Dave, and Eileen at the beach

Ravenous afterward, we settled down to a picnic dinner. Aunt Molly had everything set up at the picnic table. She brought some of her famous breaded pork chops and potato salad for the meal. Good food was an important part of our life. I loved to eat her delicious, home-cooked food, which was as good as she was. Also, by this time, my food war was over—the doctor had given me permission to eat what I wanted and when I wanted.

On Sundays, Uncle Leonard picked us up again and brought us over to their house. As we grew older, we took a bus to Aunt Molly and Uncle Leonard's. When Eileen was eleven and I was twelve, we would ride the bus after Mass on Sundays and arrive around noon. Again I anticipated the fun of the day. Uncle Leonard had the croquet game set up in the backyard. We played vigorous games of croquet—enjoying sailing the opponent's ball through the wicket and then across the yard every time we got the chance.

Then Aunt Molly brought out a delicious lunch/dinner of breaded chicken and potato salad—and, her specialty, homemade cheese cake. She was an outstanding cook—our whole family was. We had a picnic in the backyard. We all savored not only the food but also the conversation and the joking around. Aunt Molly and Uncle Leonard knew how to laugh, tease, and joke. Unlike other people I knew, they knew how to see the joyfulness and humor in the simplest things in life.

Every summer, the company where Uncle Leonard worked had an all day picnic at Euclid Beach Amusement Park. Eileen and I got to go. We were so excited the night before that we could hardly sleep. The morning of the picnic had games. Noon was Aunt Molly's delicious lunch. But the best was yet to come. Yes, David, Eileen, and I had free passes for the amusement rides all day. What a yearly treat! It was followed by dancing to Johnny Vadnal's Polka Band playing all evening—polka music was a large part of my childhood music memories. We as children not only enjoyed listening to this joyful, cheerful music but also loved to dance to it—often with adult partners. We waited for this day every year. Aunt Molly and Uncle Leonard included us in this every year too. They included us in a lot.

Me, Dave, and Eileen play around as teenagers.

In high school, we continued to spend all of our holidays together—Aunt Molly and Uncle Leonard made the holidays fun and enjoyable.

Aunt Molly and Uncle Leonard came to see me perform in my junior class and senior class plays. Uncle Leonard tried to teach me how to drive a car. He took me out once. At one point, he yelled, "Brake!", and I hit the gas. We went over a hill. The topic of my driving never came up again. Yet they were always very supportive and encouraging of me.

Even in college, Aunt Molly and Uncle Leonard were involved with my life. For example, one day, they drove down to Pittsburgh to visit me at Duquesne University. I was in a short musical for a sorority and fraternity competition—Fall Carnival. They stayed and attended several musicals, including mine. Aunt Molly and Uncle Leonard were so proud of me, and I felt it. I still remember that feeling. After the shows, we were led by my boyfriend, Steve, to Perkins Pancake House in Monroeville for a late dinner. Thoughtfully, Steve picked this location because it would enable Aunt Molly and Uncle Leonard to get back on the turnpike to Cleveland easily. We all had a wonderful time together that day and evening.

I was in a car accident in college. I was physically injured and received payment as compensation for the injuries. When I got the insurance money, I used part of it to buy a new car. Uncle Leonard helped me pick out a new, dark turquoise Chevy Malibu. It was sharp. He had his friend Harold drive it to Pittsburgh so I could have it. What a terrific treat. These times with Aunt Molly and Uncle Leonard were happy times. When I was with them, I felt that I had a family to belong to. Even though Aunt Molly and Uncle Leonard weren't my parents, I felt their love for me, their care for me, and their support of me. Over the years, this sustained me as much as Aunt Molly's cheese cake. I loved them very much.

Aunt Molly brought her cheese cake to every family gathering. It was greatly anticipated by all. It was so rich that you could only have a small piece at a time.

Aunt Molly's Famous, Fabulous Cheese Cake

Preheat oven to 350 degrees

Crust Ingredients:
10 graham cracker squares
½ stick of melted butter
2 T sugar

Crust Directions:
Roll crackers in a plastic bag

In a bowl, add sugar, butter, and graham crackers and mix thoroughly.

Press in an 8 x 8 square pan—bottom and ½ way up sides.

Sprinkle a little cinnamon on top.

Cheese Filling Ingredients:
1-8 oz. Philadelphia Cream Cheese
2-3 oz. Philadelphia Cream Cheese
5 eggs—add one egg at a time
½ t vanilla
¾ cup of sugar—add a little at a time

Cheese Filling Directions:
Put cream cheese in a mixing bowl and soften it by mixing it on slow or medium speed.

Add eggs one at a time.

Add sugar a little at a time and then add vanilla.

Pour mixture into crust.

Bake at 350 degrees for 30-35 minutes

Topping Ingredients:
8 oz. sour cream
2 T sugar
½ T vanilla

Topping Directions:
Mix ingredients by hand in a bowl until smooth.

When pie is cool, pour sour cream over the top.

Put in oven for 5 minutes at 475 degrees.

Let cool and serve.

Keep refrigerated.

Over a Pot of Brewed Coffee: Aunt Goldie and Uncle Ernie

Eileen

Eileen and Me

When Uncle Ernie was still single, he bought these Easter coats and tams with the corsages for Eileen and me.

Uncle Ernie was a quiet, gentle, and kind man. Aunt Goldie was the friendly talker. They were a long-lasting couple, based on years of a happy marriage. They had whatever it took. I just saw the quiet and the talkative aspects that complemented each other.

When Eileen and I were in our preadolescence, we lived with Aunt Julia and Uncle Joe. One summer, they wanted a vacation free of two children but had the care of Eileen and me. Aunt Goldie and Uncle Ernie entered the picture. They volunteered to care for us and have us visit with them for a week.

I remember that, when Uncle Ernie came home from his job as a laborer, he and Aunt Goldie sat down to a pot of freshly brewed coffee and talked together. Their coffee was always accompanied by a can of Carnation Evaporated Milk™ in the coffee. I never knew anyone else that did this.

One day, Uncle Ernie guided Eileen and me as we built a bird house to hang in a tree in their back yard. We built a simple house and painted it dark blue. We were very proud of it.

My memory of Aunt Goldie fast forwards to my first few years after graduating from college, the late 1960s. I would drive into East Cleveland particularly to talk with Aunt Goldie. She would talk with me about the family—something no one else would do. I always appreciated her frankness and candor. I also was impressed with the fact that she brought their children up using the book by Doctor Benjamin Spock, quite revolutionary at the time.

*Aunt Goldie and Uncle Ernie with their twins,
Karen and Kathy*

Yes, Aunt Goldie and Uncle Ernie stressed what was simple and essential in life: communication. I too valued that. Whether over a pot of coffee in the kitchen or over a ginger ale in the living room, conversation always flowed freely at the home of Aunt Goldie and Uncle Ernie.

Hungarian Chicken Paprikash

This was a favorite of the whole family and a delicious meal to be enjoyed with wonderful conversations around the table.

Ingredients:
1 small onion
cooking oil
1 T paprika
½ t black pepper
1 ½ c water
3-4 lbs. chicken cut up
flour for roux, or sour cream

Directions:
In a deep pot, sauté onion until cooked but not browned.

Add salt to taste, pepper, and paprika. Stir together.

Add chicken. Turn until warmed on all sides, about 20 minutes.

Add just enough water to cover the chicken.

Cover the pot and cook slowly over a low flame approximately 1 ½ hours.

When all pieces are tender, remove chicken and set it aside.

Make a roux of flour and water in a small bowl or shake in a jar.

Slowly stir the roux into the liquid until the broth has thickened to the desired consistency.

Sour cream can be used in place of the roux to thicken the broth.

Dumplings for Paprikash:

Ingredients:
½ t salt
½ c. milk
½ c. flour
2 eggs

Directions:
Beat eggs, salt, and milk.

Stir in flour gradually.

Drop dough into boiling water ½ t at a time.

Dumplings will rise to the top when they are cooked.

Remove the dumplings.

Add dumplings to the pot of thickened broth.

Pour the gravy and dumplings in a separate bowl and serve hot. Place chicken on a separate plate and serve on the side.

Childhood Shenanigans: Eileen

*Eileen and me in play clothes
and ready for play*

When my sister Eileen and I were children growing up, we were like twins even though we were a year apart. I was one year older than she. Well, we looked different. She had brown hair, big brown eyes, and a sturdy build. I had blond hair, blue eyes, was a little bit taller, and very skinny. But the twin part was that we did everything together. In the summer, Eileen and I played together all day long—well into our school age years. Every day was a new play adventure.

We loved to play, and we played outdoors all day, every day we could if the weather allowed. Now, even though we always played together, we welcomed anyone from the neighborhood who wanted to join us. On one specific occasion in the summer of 1954, Greg joined us. He was short, thin, had dark hair, and was eight-years-old. He liked play adventures too. At this time, Eileen was eight-years-old, and I was nine.

We had a creek near our house, across a railroad trestle, through a cemetery, and in a Metropolitan Park in Cleveland. The creek was on the other side of the cemetery and through some woods with a large spread of sassafras trees. The creek wandered through the whole woods, but we only waded in one part—and we all knew how to swim. There was a small island on this part of the creek. The island was shale rising above the creek with no growth on it. On this day, the three of us got an idea.

We all ran home to Greg's house and asked his mother if she had any hot dogs. She had some frozen ones. She asked if we wanted her to cook them. We refused and left with the package of hot dogs. I had already picked up some matches somewhere. We ran back to the island in excitement. We built a campfire of dry wood branches we found around the island and roasted hot dogs using green tree limbs. I don't remember how we got the limbs off the trees.

What a delight! The hot dogs were delicious—better than we had ever had. We actually thought we were so clever as to fool Greg's mother. Of course, we didn't fool her. I just can't figure out still why she gave us the hot dogs. I guess she wanted us to have a play adventure too. And we were gutsy women even then. We were proud of our sense of adventure and fun with the outdoors.

Roasted Hot Dogs

Ingredients:
Hot Dogs—preferably borrowed
A hot, teepee fire
Green limbs from trees—one per person

Directions:
Place the hot dog on the limb.

Roast on the fire.

Enjoy.

Nurturer and Consulting Chef: Aunt Margie

Aunt Margie with me
as a young child of five years

My mother could not care for me as a child. From a young age, Aunt Margie was a caregiver. When I was four and five-years-old and my aunt Margie was in high school, she had a bedroom which she shared with me and my sister, Eileen. Each night, we had a ritual: Eileen and I lay down on the double bed, and Aunt Margie played the record player. The song I remember was "Little Jimmy Brown." I don't know why I liked it so much or why I remember it, but I do. It was just a simple ballad about Little Jimmy Brown, who was born, grew up, married, and died in a small town.

I don't have a lot of memories from my early childhood, partly because I was young and partly because they were troubling times in some ways. But I have some recollections from my earliest childhood when I lived with my Hungarian/German grandpa. Aunt Margie lived there too.

When I was five, Aunt Margie was only 15 years old, but she was a caretaker even then. For example, she rubbed my chest with Vick's Vaporub™ when I had a cold and tucked me into bed at night.

We used to sometimes tease Aunt Margie— Eileen and I—and call her "Aunt Dodgey." I don't really know why. I guess it was a kid thing. We giggled, and she just smiled at us.

Aunt Margie walked Eileen and me to school at St. Patrick's every day when I was in first grade and Eileen was in kindergarten. The year before, when I was in kindergarten, she walked just me to school. Then she walked herself to high school. That was very protective of her.

At festivals at St. Wendelin's where she went to high school, Aunt Margie wore beautiful Hungarian costumes and danced the ritual dances for various holidays and celebrations. As I recall, they were white dresses with a fitted bodice and a flared, full skirt. There was beautiful, colorful embroidery on the hem on the bottom and the top apron. She looked lovely in them.

During these years, on Decoration Day and Labor Day, there was a parade that passed our house when we all lived on Monroe with Grandpa. Grandpa, in his wheel chair, hung the flag on the porch and

Eileen, Aunt Margie, and I joined him to watch the parade march down the street and into the cemetery across the street. Then the soldiers did a 21-gun salute to the veterans. The whole ceremony was quite exciting and moving.

Aunt Margie had her own set of losses. Her mother died when she was seven, and her father died when she was 17. Yet she still was a caregiver and a nurturer.

Now, that I was an adult, we conversed about cooking. Aunt Margie was a nurturer, and one way that she did this was through cooking. I loved to hear her tips—she had learned them over many years while she had become an extraordinary cook. She was eager and enthusiastic to talk about cooking and full of knowledge.

Aunt Margie carried on the tradition of the Hungarian cooking taught by Grandma and Grandpa and passed on by my mother, Aunt Molly, and Aunt Julia. So, for example, she reminded me of how to make egg dumplings, stuffed cabbage, cabbage and noodles, chicken paprikash, and Grandpa's chicken and beef soup. And, she passed on Aunt Molly's famous and fabulous cheese cake recipe. Of course, Uncle Bernie helped her with the cooking, so he deserved some credit for these scrumptious meals.

Aunt Margie always enjoyed a good joke and a laugh and was fastidious about keeping everything neat and clean.

Epilogue: In 2012, hospice said Aunt Margie had only a few days to a week to live—she had been declining for quite a while. I drove to Cleveland to be with her. I was at her bedside with her husband, Uncle Bernie, her two sons, Bernie and Bob, and her two grandchildren, Natalie and Maria, when she died. It was unclear to me whether I would be comfortable with this experience. I surprised myself as I began talking to Aunt Margie. Although I wasn't sure if she heard me, I talked to her about all of my childhood memories and my cooking memories. I told her I loved her. She died peacefully, and I was glad to be there to say goodbye.

One year earlier, I had volunteered to work with Family Hospice using art with children and adolescents who were dealing with imminent or recent loss. At the last minute, I got scared and backed out. I had suffered so many losses as a child and adolescent that I was afraid hospice work would just stir up troubling memories better left at rest.

However, after being with Aunt Margie at her death, I realized that life experience and therapy had brought me to another place. I could handle hospice, I believed. I came back from Cleveland and called Family Hospice to ask if the volunteer services manager would reconsider accepting me as a volunteer. I was welcomed back. I began my volunteer work by doing art with children and adolescents at three full day Camp Healing Heart events starting June 2 of that year.

When I was growing up, no one ever talked about uncomfortable or unpleasant happenings in my family. That's how it was in most families at the time. Therefore, I never talked about all of my losses. It took years of therapy as an adult to deal with these issues of loss and abandonment. Through art, I hope to facilitate the communication of feelings around the personal losses of these children and adolescents' as they grow and develop in healthy way.

Coconut Bars

Aunt Margie loved to bake, and her favorite recipe was for coconut squares. Everyone in our family grew to look forward to there being a dessert at every family event. It is a simple but delicious recipe.

Ingredients:
1 white cake box mix
1 24-oz. bottle of Hershey's™ chocolate sauce
1 package shredded coconut

Directions:
Prepare the white cake box mix according to directions on the box. Bake in a 9" x 13" pan.

When the cake is cool, cut into 2" x 3" rectangles and place on a cookie sheet or in another container so that bars are not touching each other.

Place in the freezer and allow to freeze.

Place chocolate sauce and coconut into two separate bowls.

Dip each bar of cake in chocolate sauce until completely coated.

Transfer chocolate-coated bar to coconut flakes. Roll to coat bar completely.

As before, place bars on a cookie sheet or in another container so that bars are not touching.

Refrigerate until serving.

Eating Out: Current Adventures of Eileen and Ellen

Eileen and me enjoying a beverage together in a coffee shop in Gainesville, Florida

As I mentioned, Eileen and I were orphans of a sort. But, through it all, Eileen and I stuck together.

Throughout our lives, we enjoyed being active. As children, we played vigorously with each other and often with neighbors. We waded in the creek; made homemade fishing poles; built campfires and roasted frozen hot dogs; jumped rope—double Dutch; rode buses to swimming, ice skating, and roller skating. Each day, waking up was an event, an unplanned and unknown adventure. We had busy childhoods, full of activity, which helped keep us afloat in the midst of a life of change, loss, sadness and anxiety. We used that emotional energy to create wonderful play ideas that were fun and also made powerful feelings more manageable.

However, as adults, we have lived far apart for our entire lives. Despite a great geographical distance between Eileen and me, we are emotionally close. I love my sister and really miss that we do not live in the same city. Every time we end our visit and I leave her, as I walk away from her and toward the plane in Gainesville, I get teary-eyed. I begin missing my sister immediately. Yet we also talk on the phone weekly for an hour or more. We discuss things great and small—my retirement, her retirement, my Osher classes, her children and grandchildren, food, and our readings. Eileen has moved around from time to time and has ended her wanderings in Gainesville, Florida. We take yearly turns visiting one another in Gainesville and in Pittsburgh. We continue to have an evolving relationship.

In the summer of 2010, Eileen came to visit twice: for my retirement party and to treat me to a 65th birthday in New York City. I was delighted with both. She was a significant part of why the retirement party was so memorable. New York City was great fun too. We drove to Carlisle, Pennsylvania, to visit my friend, Janet, and take the train from Harrisburg to New York City's Penn Station. We were so excited on the train that the time seemed to pass slowly. But the train was also exciting because we so rarely rode one.

We were told we'd be fine in New York City if we didn't act like tourists. We came up and out of Penn Station to the street level at 5:00 PM—to all of the rushing people and neon lights and racing cars. We stopped to look in amazement. We exclaimed, "Can you believe this? Isn't this terrific—and exciting!" How could we not look like tourists? We were tourists! And we continued to be tourists as we went to see the hit Broadway play at the time, "Wicked," which was more passionate and powerful than any musical that I had ever seen. We took the ferry to and from Ellis Island and past the Statue of Liberty—a moving experience because it called forth the immense number of immigrant people that came to this country for freedom and a chance at a better life, and our grandparents were two of them. Greenwich Village was a disappointment. It was hard to imagine what was so significant about the place today as we just roamed some of the streets indiscriminately.

Macy's was a posh department store that mostly reminded us of the Thanksgiving Day parades we watched on TV. Then there was 5th Avenue and Broadway, exciting markers of the New York City we had only heard of before. Now we were walking and roaming these streets. We went to "Good Morning, America" which Eileen has been watching for over 40 years in the hopes to wave and be seen on TV, but we were not. Yet we enjoyed being in the large group of fans outside the studio. We ducked into souvenir shops to purchase I love New York t-shirts and coffee mugs as presents for ourselves and others. We even took wild cab rides, holding on to the door handles to avoid sliding off of the seat and onto the floor. We were tourists and sightseers, and we loved every minute of sharing it together. Busy and active, we were enthralled with the wonder of New York City. We still did adventure very well together.

We have come a long way from being two orphaned children. We have emerged as two independent women sightseeing in New York City, who are sisters, friends, and welcoming travel companions. But we are also learning how to be dependent on each other—in a healthy way—as sisters should be.

Eileen and me joking around, enjoying each other's company

In 2011, Eileen and I had a wonderful sisters' vacation together staying in a comfortable condominium in St. Augustine, Florida. The condo at St. Augustine Tennis and Racquet Club was near the ocean but still a short drive. There was a pool near every few buildings. Eileen treated me to this vacation since I was short on funds and could only come up with enough Frequent Flyer Miles to get myself down to Florida. We were committed to having one vacation a year together. I felt very fortunate that Eileen essentially gave me this vacation with her. She's a generous sister.

Our daily adventure began with a routine. We had a breakfast of an English muffin and peanut butter and coffee and then went to the beach by 9:00 AM. In St. Augustine, we were beach lovers. We dragged the umbrellas, chairs, and cooler from the car, through the sand, and onto the beach. It was not easy, but it was necessary. We were determined—and we struggled together as a team. Then Eileen and I set up. With the cooler's beverages and snacks, we were ready for a wonderful morning where we could look at the ocean, talk, sip a cool bottle of water, eat a piece of fruit, and take a dip in the ocean from time to time. I even rode a bike on the ocean's edge and was delighted that I could still do so even if not for very long. Soon, Eileen's friends, Mika and Clair, who are very comfortable to be with, joined us. We talked and laughed in the sun beside the ocean. I not only had the opportunity to share this time with Eileen but also to enjoy the company of her good friends.

In the afternoon, we returned to the condo for a lunch—maybe a salad and some fruit—and then went out to the pool, which was an inviting temperature. We spent about two hours there. Mika and Clair often joined us. Mika and I talked while Clair swam. Lee Ann, Eileen's daughter, and Madelyn, Eileen's granddaughter, visited for a few days and stayed with us in our condo. It was a little crowded but fun—kind of a party. For a few days, Silvia, Thien, and Emilie also rented a condo and joined us at the pool and ocean from time to time. Silvia is Eileen's lifelong friend. Just like me, Eileen has cultivated good and loyal friends, who are the family she never had. We both had accrued a wonderful collection of other sisters.

In the late afternoon, we'd all come into the condo and rest, taking naps or just relaxing and talking. Often, for dinner, we would cook and eat in. One night Mika cooked a scrumptious spaghetti and meat sauce dinner with garlic bread and salad. During this week, the temperatures reached highs of 100 degrees or so, thus, going sightseeing in the city was not an appealing option. But one night, we ventured out to eat at a favorite restaurant, A1A, on one of the main drags in St. Augustine. All nine of us were together, gathered in friendship and enjoying delicious food, the beach, and lively conversation.

The last day, Eileen proposed that just she and I go out to a breakfast early to see the sun rise over the bay at Mary's, a small, quaint restaurant across the street from the bay. I was so delighted that she wanted to spend time with just me before I left. We got the prized table in front of the window and watched a vibrant orange and red glowing bay as the sun came up from the horizon. Over our breakfasts of bacon and eggs, toast, coffee, and sliced tomatoes, we shared the last morning of our vacation together. Like the sun rising, our relationship was emerging—a new attentiveness to each other. The week at St. Augustine's with Eileen was a joyful week. I felt very close to her.

In 2012, Eileen visited up north. First, she stayed with our cousin, Bernie, and his wife, Felicia, and their two daughters. The high school graduation party that called us all together was a wonderful opportunity for the seven cousins to visit. It was fun to be together and get to know each other a bit better—we all live a distance apart and have not kept in touch. That's how my family is. But, when together, we really liked and enjoyed each other.

Then Eileen came for a four-day stay in Pittsburgh. She remained with me and asked if we could have a little less activity, a very unusual request from someone who liked to be on the move. However, she explained that she had come from a busy end of the school year at work and an active visit with Bernie and Felicia and would like some down time.

My dear friends enjoy Eileen when she visits, and we have fun together in Pittsburgh. We began our Pittsburgh adventure that year when my friends, Sandie, Dee, and Martha, ate dinner at River Towne Pour House in Monroeville, a micro-brewery that also serves gigantic, wonderful grilled chicken salads. It is a joy being with Eileen and my good friends, who are very welcoming.

You know, I am Eileen's only sister, and it was like us against the world. However, now we enjoy each other's company as well as the company of each other's friends during our visits together. This time we also talked about what she will do next year, about finances in retirement, and health care.

We conversed about movies—watching them is her favorite pastime—and went to see two of them. Eileen exclaimed, "I am going through movie withdrawal because I haven't seen a movie in ten days!" When we shopped for clothes for me, she said, "I like spending other people's money." This year, I felt as if Eileen and I were becoming even more at home with and accepting of the person each of us had become.

My most recent visits with Eileen have been filled with activity as usual. Life really is one small adventure after another for us. But we are no longer the sad little girls, who used adventure to cope with the change, loss, sadness, and anxiety of our young lives. We have come a long way, baby! We embrace full and active lives, rich in the joy and delight of simple things—with each other, with others, and in the doing—purely for their pleasure.

Stuffed Cabbage

Eileen has chosen to include her stuffed cabbage recipe here. Although she and I have many similarities in our recipes (see Richard's story for mine), Eileen has her own identifying version based on how she has refined the recipe over the years. Notice her addition of kielbasa and sauerkraut in hers. Hers is also a delicious recipe.

Ingredients:
2 cabbages
2 lbs. ground beef
1 c. rice (not Minute Rice ™)
1 large chopped onion
salt and pepper
garlic powder, generously sprinkled over the meat mixture
3 eggs
1 46-oz. bottle tomato juice (Keep an extra bottle on hand to thin the mix if needed.)
1 10¾-oz. can tomato soup
1 15-oz. can tomato sauce
1 14-oz. can of Bavarian sauerkraut
1 lb. Kielbasa, cut into 1" slices

Directions:
Cut around the stems of the two cabbages.

In a large pot, boil the cabbages only enough to loosen their leaves.

Remove 20-25 of the largest leaves, keeping them whole.

Slice remaining cabbage into sauerkraut-type, or slightly thicker, slices.

Keep 4 inches of cabbage water in the pot. Pour out the rest. Mix in tomato sauce.

Fill 1/3 of leaf with raw meat filling (meat, rice, seasoning), roll shut, stuff ends inside of roll.

Put rolls in large pot with cabbage water. Add tomato juice, tomato soup, and sliced cabbage. Simmer 2 hours, adding additional tomato juice as needed.

Add Bavarian sauerkraut and kielbasa to the top. Simmer an addition 1-2 hours.

Serve with parsley potatoes or mashed potatoes and French bread.

Yield: 15 medium-sized cabbage rolls

Soul Sister, Country-Western Style: Lee-Ann

Lee-Ann enjoys her princess-style wedding dress.

Eileen adopted Lee-Ann and her sister Anita when they were five-and four-years–old, respectively. Lee-Ann has always seen me as her soul sister. She likes to talk a lot, enjoys being very social, and can be quite independent. This sounds familiar.

Lee-Ann has a great sense of humor. She is funny, and she likes to tease. She is a delight to be around. Lee-Ann is married to Mark; he too has a wonderful sense of humor. The two of them together can be like a comedy team, entertaining everyone around them.

Lee-Ann is a pretty blond with an impish smile. She is comfortable in jeans and cowboy boots, a real country-western person. However, to everyone's surprise, for her wedding, Lee-Ann wore a beautiful princess-style dress. I guess some dreams just never die. She looked beautiful too. But she and Mark served barbequed chicken at the reception. You simply can't take the country-western out of the person.

She is so proud of her daughter, Madelyn. Madelyn was born prematurely due to Lee-Ann's brittle diabetes. She survived and thrived due to the good care of Lee-Ann, Mark, their families and friends, and the staff of Shands Hospital. Madelyn was a poster child for the March of Dimes when she was one year old. Lee-Ann shows her pride as a mother in many ways. She frequently emails me photos of Madelyn at school, in dance recitals, or building with LEGOs™. Lee-Ann is very attentive to Madelyn and her development of social skills as Lee Ann makes sure that Madelyn is always in attendance at preschool, in swimming lessons, and at dance class—all which Madelyn loves. It is a delight to see.

I call Lee-Ann "Little Lee-Ann" because I use the diminutive to express fondness for a person—I'm not sure why, but I've been doing that for years. Little Lee-Ann is very dear to me and a wonderful niece. I feel honored that she would see me as her soul sister.

Five-Bean Chili

Lee-Ann learned to make a five-bean chili while she was in the Girl Scouts. Here is her delightful recipe:

Ingredients:
1 lb. ground beef
1 onion, chopped
1 28-oz. can stewed tomatoes
1 bottle Masterpiece Original Barbeque Sauce™
1 can each: pinto beans, pork-n-beans, lima beans, kidney beans, and navy beans

Directions:
In a large pot, brown ground beef and chopped onion. Drain fat.

Add stewed tomatoes, barbeque sauce, and beans.

Bring the mixture to a boil. Reduce heat simmer for 1 hour.

Hints from Early Childhood: Anita

Pictured with her family, Anita treasures being a wife and mother.

Eileen's other adopted daughter, my niece, Anita, seemed to practice for motherhood all of her life. She was adopted at four-years-old along with her five-year-old sister, Lee-Ann. From her youngest years, Anita took caring for her dolls very seriously. She would bathe them, feed them, burp them, and tuck them into bed. I often observed this frequent routine. Anita was the most loving little mother to her dolls.

When she grew old enough, Anita continued this behavior in real life. As I observed her babysit, I could see these same loving and caring traits in her as she tended to the children in her care. Likewise, Anita would interact with the child she was caring for, talking and explaining what was occurring and why. It was a delight to see such attention to the small ones. Anita obviously respected every child.

Anita also played well with the children she babysat. She engaged each child in fun activities. She clearly delighted in connecting with them and bringing out every child's best. Anita never grew impatient with children. She was remarkable really.

Anita struggled in high school and experienced some difficult times, but she was always successful in her relationships to children. That never changed. Whether the children were neighbors' children or children of my sister's friends, Anita was always adept at working with them.

Now she has children of her own and is a caring and attentive mother. She was meant to be a mother really and is truly happy about this role and serious about accepting its responsibilities. Anita's first child, Lila Marie, lives with her dad in New Mexico and loves riding horses. She sees Anita and her grandmother, Eileen, as often as she can. Anita lives joyfully as a wife and mother with her other children, Montana and Shelby, and her husband, Jade, in Utah. I am happy that Anita is my niece and proud of the life that she has made for herself.

Sweet Potato Casserole

As Anita says about herself and her recipe, "It's me: southern and sweet."

Ingredients:
butter (for casserole dish)
3 lbs. sweet potatoes, peeled and cubed
1 4.5-oz. can evaporated milk
½ c. brown sugar
5 T unsalted butter, melted
1 t vanilla extract
½ t ground cinnamon
2 eggs, beaten
1 cup mini marshmallows
½ cup sweetened, shredded coconut
¼ cup chopped cashews or almonds
salt and pepper to taste

Directions:
Preheat oven to 350 degrees.

Butter a two-quart casserole dish and set aside.

Add the sweet potatoes to a large pot of cold, salted water. Bring to a boil and simmer for about 20 minutes. Drain sweet potatoes in a colander.

Mash potatoes in a large bowl. Add evaporated milk, brown sugar, butter, vanilla, cinnamon, eggs, salt, and pepper.

Mix until smooth. Pour in casserole dish. Bake for 25-30 minutes.

In a small bowl, toss the cashews, coconut, and marshmallows.

Remove the casserole from the oven. Top with cashew mixture.

Bake until marshmallows are lightly toasted, about 10-15 minutes.

Cool 5 minutes before serving.

We Continue to Talk: Part 1: Janet

Janet in her garden that she loved in Mt. Lebanon

I have known Janet since I was 17-years-old, and I am now 68. She is my oldest and dearest friend. When I was admitted to Duquesne University, she was assigned as my big sister, which meant that we would get to know each other by corresponding in letters throughout the summer before I began college. Thus, I would know one person when I arrived at Duquesne. On campus, she would orient me to college life from her perspective. Who would have known that we would become—and remain—close friends for five decades?

I loved receiving her handwritten, fountain-pen-inked letters from Puerto Rico—how thrilling for me. Janet was so caring, kind and sensitive to me, a beginner in college. She described the urban campus to me from the ability to walk easily downtown or ride streetcars into Oakland. She wrote about talks in the grottos with friends or with the Holy Ghost Fathers, who would be taking a stroll. She acknowledged the rigorous studies, and she highlighted the friendships that she had made. While she received letters from "Ellen," my name was listed as "Ellen Jane" on her information from Duquesne. When we finally met, I was not the "Ellen Jane" that she had envisioned. In fact, we were both very different from each other's imaginings. Janet was a college intellectual and a member of the Cosmopolitan Club. My relatives were strict in high school, so, in contrast, I intended to socialize at college. I became a sorority girl and enjoyed my freedom.

Although we were different in many ways, we continued to relate. Both of us were open to developing at least a casual friendship. Bound by our shared financial struggle to get through college, we continued to keep in touch from time to time during the four years. During any given semester, we would each discuss the sharing of any extra money we received from scholarships and loans with the other person. We never needed to do so—we each always managed on our own financially—but we always offered to help each other. Also, because we both were accepting of a variety of people, we enjoyed visiting with each other, different though we were. When she visited me, Janet often brought friends of hers, like Sue who was British born but spent her adolescence in West Virginia. I kept Janet apprised of my roommate and friend, Mary Fran, who was also from West Virginia. We continued our relationship in this casual vein.

After college, Janet went to Spain for an adventurous semester, and I was finishing my first semester of my senior year and awaiting student teaching. The second semester, Janet returned to Pittsburgh and got an apartment in Oakland and a job teaching Spanish at Bishop Boyle High School in Homestead. She invited me to move in with her for financial reasons, and I accepted. I would be student teaching in secondary English at Taylor Allderdice High School in Squirrel Hill—a bus ride away. It was quite exciting to live in an apartment, and it helped me settle what I would do after I graduated. Until then, I had no idea what my future would be and was just anxious about it—I avoided all conversation.

Our apartment was a small, typical, slightly shabby Oakland apartment with a bright blue rug in the living room and a cheap couch and chair. A swinging half-door separated the living room from the bedroom. The bedroom had a dresser, a double bed for Janet, and a single bed by a window for me. Off of the living room was the old but functional kitchen with the exit out of the apartment. Janet and I had some of our best conversations in that kitchen about what we wanted in our families when we married—we had plans. On Sunday mornings, Janet always cooked delicious bacon and eggs—and we talked. This is how our friendship really developed.

We talked about creating the family we never had—one with stability and love apparent. Conversation ensued about cooking tantalizing meals and being attentive to our families in ways that we had never experienced. I had learned to cook well although my home environment was often not warm and caring. Janet had never really learned to cook. Both of us were left to our own designs growing up. Yes, we had learned by default what we did not want, and we would do better. Janet and I were discovering the things we had in common. Even our apartment attire was compatible. Janet had a turquoise, patterned muumuu, and I had a turquoise, cut off hospital gown. We were quite the roommate combination.

I should have learned how to get a man from rooming with Janet. Janet met Dan at Bishop Boyle and married him. She knew how to pick a good man. She would play Spanish love songs on the record player while she talked to Dan on the phone. It always sounded like a party was happening. Janet bought a guitar and asked Dan to teach her how to play guitar— she never played it once after they got married. Janet also encouraged Dan to move out of his mother's house and into an apartment rooming with a friend, Joe. She had her strategies, and they worked.

A number of people from Pittsburgh flew down to Puerto Rico to be with them at the wedding. My sister and I flew down too. Imagine flying to Puerto Rico on December 26th from wintery Pittsburgh. It was beautiful in Aguadilla—white beaches, a pristine ocean and sugar cane fields. It seemed very exotic and romantic.

Soon Janet was living in Dormont and, then, Mt. Lebanon and beginning a family—a daughter followed by a son. One Christmas while living in Dormont, Janet and Dan did not have a Christmas tree. I carried my tree down a flight of stairs and brought my live, fully decorated Christmas tree over to them in my VW bug—I was going away for Christmas. The tree barely fit in my beetle, limbs and bulbs sticking out of the window, but it arrived in one piece. Dan carried it up a flight of stairs into their apartment, and it looked very festive in their living room.

During these times, we talked on the phone often.

Janet was creating the kind of family she had never had. I was invited to her home to join in the celebration of life and enjoy the delicious food. She cooked Puerto Rican food like red beans and rice as a side dish for tasty chicken and salad. But Janet was described by her mother as "my American daughter," and she also created elaborate, traditional Thanksgiving dinners, for example, with turkey and all of the trimmings. Also, she always introduced a new side dish at each holiday meal. Janet became quite an extraordinary cook. She also sewed, baked, and cooked daily while still teaching high school Spanish full time. She enjoyed creating a nurturing and caring home for Dan, Jennifer, and Joel—and, of course, herself. This was her top priority. And, she was willing to share her family with me.

Janet has done a wonderful job building the family life for herself that we talked about over Sunday breakfasts in our Oakland apartment so many years ago. Janet, Dan and the kids—and the grandchildren—are close, caring, and connected. Janet and I grew through these times and continue to grow in our friendship.

Red Beans and Rice

This simple Puerto Rican treat is tasty with a salad and a pork chop.

Ingredients:
115-oz. can medium or light kidney beans, undrained
¼ c. tomato sauce
2 T minced green pepper
1 T olive oil

Directions:
Put all the ingredients together in a saucepan and cook for 20 minutes on low heat.

Add garlic powder or salt as desired. Mixture should be slightly runny.

Serve over long grain rice.

We Continue to Talk: Part 2: Janet

Janet now in Carlisle, Pennsylvania—just a frequent phone call away

When Janet's children were in high school, she and I began meeting at the European Health Spa in Green Tree on Friday nights. We would tolerate exercise so that we could go in the sauna and whirlpool and relax and talk for quite a while. Then, we would go to the Ground Round Restaurant next door, talk some more and eat greasy, fattening food—totally defeating our purpose in exercising. We were thin then. We talked about the men I was dating, and she would give her helpful insights. We would also converse about her children and adolescence—a favorite topic of mine.

When I was a graduate student working on my doctorate, we would frequently meet in Mt. Lebanon at Friday's and enjoy lunch and conversation. I often talked about my anxiety over collecting the data. I had special education teachers facilitate story writing with emotionally troubled adolescents and then respond with empathy to the stories. Being a little paranoid during the collection of data process, I always worried that a student in the study might commit suicide and my stories would be blamed as the cause. I also was very anxious about the oral exam. Janet would listen patiently. Free-spirited Janet ordered something new off the menu every time, but I, always on a diet, ordered a grilled chicken sandwich and ate it with half the bun. We talked some about important things but mostly about casual things. Janet helped me keep more balanced; I can be too serious.

Once, we even met at my home on Chislett Street in Morningside and drove to Shadyside to eat at a Greek restaurant. We were dressed quite fashionably and looked like stylish, middle-aged women. I wore a turquoise, long-sleeved, silk blouse, a brown, fitted straight skirt, and high, high heels with straps around the ankle. Janet dressed equally as fashionably. We sat at a table overlooking Walnut Street and enjoyed more good conversation and some wine with our meal of lamb-stuffed grape leaves, hummus and pita bread, and a Greek salad. Nurturing our friendship with food and conversation was a theme in our ongoing relationship. We continued to talk about men, my doctoral studies, and the ongoing independence of her children.

When I had some bad times, Janet was always supportive and encouraging. She always saw my strengths and focused on them. She always talked to me caringly and practically and strived toward solving the problem. During the times that I was hospitalized on a psychiatric unit, Janet visited and called. The food wasn't present, but the camaraderie was. Janet and my other friend, Sue, would transform my room into a dorm room. Laughter and gaiety abounded. Janet always had the ability to listen, empathize, and problem-solve, with a heavy emphasis on problem-solving.

During one of my hospitalizations, my sister could not even talk to me on the phone. She was too overwhelmed, upset, and scared for me—remember our mother had been hospitalized for 13 years. Janet became the intermediary, who would talk to my sister, reassuring her of my progress. Janet was very encouraging and continued to be a good and loyal friend throughout. We continued to talk. I lost my job when I was hospitalized the third time. It was against the law, but I felt beaten down and unable to fight for myself. Janet and three other friends paid for my hospitalization until I got another job.

Five years ago, Janet moved to Carlisle, Pennsylvania—over 200 miles away. I worried about our friendship surviving, but I didn't need to. We have continued to have long, weekly conversations on the phone about all things. We also visit from time to time. Janet has come to call me her other sister, and I feel that she is my other sister. I am grateful for her friendship.

I have eaten many Puerto Rican meals that are delicious when I have visited Janet at her home. This is a favorite of mine, so I was delighted when she chose to select this as her recipe.

Arroz Con Pollo

Ingredients:
2 lbs. of chicken pieces or whole chicken, cut up
2 14.5-oz. cans of chicken broth
½ green pepper, diced
1 onion, diced
4 cloves of garlic, diced or crushed
1 15-oz. can of tomato sauce
Adobo seasoning (found in seasoning section)
2 c. white rice
1 T olive oil
2 pkg. Sõzan Goya (found in the international foods
   section of the grocery store)

Directions:
Stew chicken in broth with green pepper and onion.
Add garlic and tomato sauce. Cook until the meat falls
off the bone.

Season with salt and adobo. When the chicken is
cooked until it is tender, add white rice and olive oil.

If you can find Sõzan Goya, add 2 packs to the sauce at
the same time (This will turn the rice lovely golden
color).

Serve a side salad of lettuce, tomato, etc., tossed in a
vinaigrette, olive oil dressing. In Puerto Rico, tostones
are also served. They can be bought in the supermarket
in the frozen food section where the international foods
or Goya products are located. They are already sliced
and just have to be fried.

Aromas and Aromas: Me

*Me with Janet, one person who strongly influenced me
to start cooking in retirement*

I was consumed by my teaching of preschool, high
school, and college for 34 years—and I loved it. I still
found time for doing fun things with friends, like going
out to eat often, but rarely found time to cook. Also I
was single and without a family during this time, so I
didn't need to cook. I could go to restaurants and enjoy
being cooked for and served. At home, I did make my
usual Shake-n-Bake chicken, baked potato, and
vegetable; or Shake-n-Bake pork tenderloin, baked
potato, and vegetable; or chicken vegetable soup; or
chili. It was not very creative, but it did sustain me and
required limited time and effort.

Then I decided to retire at age 65. Janet gave me
a cookbook, *Best of the Best One Dish*, by Publications
International Ltd., 2009, as a retirement present.
Hesitantly, I decided to investigate the book. I could
not imagine getting that involved in cooking. To my
surprise, I loved it. Also, the recipes within took time

but were basic and thus doable for me—a novice in cooking. I loved the chopping, dicing, and slicing—and the aroma of celery, onions, red peppers, and green peppers that filled the rooms. I enjoyed the cooking process and felt the joy of nurturing my guests. I loved cooking for friends. The recipes from the book are delicious and care for the soul. One recipe, Home Style Skillet Chicken, is a tasty, hearty dinner, especially on fall or winter evenings.

I also took a course in the University of Pittsburgh's Osher Life Long Learning Program from cook, Al Kosmal, called Soups, Soups, and More Soups. I was introduced to ten soups most of which were new to me. Of the ten, my favorites are the Carrot and Orange Soup, the Elegant Pimento Soup, the East European Chick Pea Soup, Vichyssoise, and the Spinach Risotto Soup. I was enthusiastic about them so I cooked most of them, one a weekend, often for my friends too. I even took the Carrot and Orange Soup to a party, and it was a hit. People asked for the recipe. I have served the Elegant Pimento Soup and Carrot and Orange Soup at small dinner parties, and both were successful additions to the menu. Finally, the East European Chick Pea Soup went with nine of us camping. With its ingredients of beef sausage, diced tomatoes, and spinach, it was a hearty, tasty dinner when we first arrived and set up camp.

In general, I find myself planning the menu for days ahead and shopping frequently for small amounts of food like Europeans do—I enjoy shopping for food. I anticipate the cooking with pleasure and delight. For me, this is a plus of retirement—discovering that I thrive on cooking. Who would have thought this career woman would feel passionate about cooking? My collection of recipes is growing at a rapid rate.

In my wooden recipe box are index cards with recipes that I've gathered over the years—not a lot for as old as I am. I've not been into cooking for long periods of time.

One favorite recipe is for a scrumptious pecan pie. The filling includes unwhipped whipping cream, but the magic ingredient is brandy. I am loyal to my Catholic heritage and use Christian Brothers brandy. The pie is always a hit. When I taught high school in the early and mid-1970s and the school district called a snow day, I would stay up late and bake a pecan pie. The next afternoon, in my blue Volkswagen bug, which could trudge through any snow, I would drive around delivering slices to my friends. This is not a healthy recipe but rather a decadent one to be reserved for celebratory occasions. It became a snow day ritual. I love rituals.

Home Style Skillet Chicken

Ingredients:
4 chicken thighs
2 T vegetable or olive oil
4 cloves garlic, minced
8 small red or new potatoes, quartered
12 pearl onions, peeled
1 c. baby carrots
2 stalks celery, cut into ½ inch pieces
½ red bell pepper, diced
2 T of cornstarch
1 c. chicken broth
½ c. sherry

Directions:
In the oil in a large skillet, brown chicken thighs on both sides.

Add chicken broth and sherry. Bring to boil.

Add carrots, cubed red pepper, minced garlic, cut up celery, pearl onions and   quartered red potatoes. Bring to a boil.

Simmer about 30 minutes with lid on. .

When everything is tender and cooked, thicken the juice for gravy with cornstarch.

Yield: 4 servings

Carrot and Orange Soup

Ingredients:
½ c. butter
½ c. olive oil
3 leeks, thinly sliced
1 lb. carrots, thinly sliced
4 c. chicken or vegetable broth
2 rinds and juice of 2 oranges
½ t freshly grated nutmeg
¼ c. plain yogurt plus extra for garnishing
fresh cilantro, chopped
salt and pepper to taste

Directions:
Melt butter with oil in large pan. Add leeks and carrots and stir well coating the vegetables. Cover and cook for about 10 minutes until the vegetables begin to soften.

Pour in the stock, orange rind, and juice. Add the nutmeg, salt, and pepper. Bring to a boil, lower heat, and simmer for about 30 minutes or until the vegetables are tender.

Leave to cool slightly.

Puree in a food processor or blender until smooth.

Return the soup to the pan and add yogurt. Reheat gently.

Ladle the soup into bowls.

Add a swirl of yogurt in the center of each. Sprinkle with the cilantro to garnish.

Serve immediately.

Yield: 6 servings.

Deluxe Pecan Pie

I got this recipe from my friend, Rosemary, who was a colleague at St. Francis Hospital.

Ingredients:
1 9" unbaked pie crust
2 T butter, melted
½ c. dark corn syrup
3 eggs
½ c. whipping cream, unwhipped
1 c. sugar
1 t vanilla
½ t salt
¼ c. of brandy
1 c. pecan halves

Directions:
Heat oven to 375 degrees.

In small mixing bowl, beat eggs and stir in sugar, salt, butter, syrup, and cream.

Stir in vanilla, brandy, and pecans.

Pour into pastry-lined pie pan.

Bake 40 to 50 minutes or until filling is set and pastry is golden.

Cool.

Yield: 8-10 servings

MAIN
COURSE

Delectable relationships sustain me and nourish me in an ongoing way.

Recipes from My Oglebay Friends

Checking in at Wilson Lodge in Oglebay Resort in West Virginia are Martha, me, Dee, and Sandie

Martha, Sandie, Dee, and I have hung out together for over 15 years. After several years of having coffee and dinners out together, going on hiking, cross-country ski or canoeing trips, we settled into yearly January retreats at Oglebay Resort in Wheeling, West Virginia. As the years passed, we added a summer retreat at Hocking Hills, Ohio, in June. Just recently, we have added an

October journey to Ligonier, Pennsylvania. We are now talking about adding a trip in the spring to North East, Pennsylvania.

However, now we are discussing trips to coincide with all of our birthdays. Thus, we would do Oglebay over the Martin Luther King, Jr., holiday weekend to celebrate Dee's January birthday. We would go to Hocking Hills in May to honor Martha's birthday. August would be our month to celebrate my birthday on the beach in Erie, Pennsylvania, and we would enjoy the leaves' changing as we celebrate Sandie's fall birthday in October in Ligonier. This is our tentative plan. We can get busy, so we are not sure if we can pull off four trips a year. Still, this is our current thought. No matter what, though, we will keep Oglebay in January and one summer trip in the works.

I have introduced this section of essays, and recipes by Sandie, Martha, Dee, and me, with a description of our Oglebay retreats in general. It shows the special bond that the four of us share. When we are together, we are our own small community with an *n* of four, but a very meaningful, vibrant group. We nurture and nourish each other through friendship and food.

- **Martha's Healthy Meal, Fast Turkey Chili**, fortified us in the winter's cold at Oglebay.

- **Sandie's Zucchini Soup** nourished us in all of our retreats, and the **Simple Pasta Sauce** proved to be a delicious recipe for me and guests.

- **Dee's Spinach Soufflé** accented one of her open house dinners.

- **My Mulligatawny Soup** warmed us all winter time.

Women Nourishing Women

Having fun enjoying the delicious food and joyful conversation at Later Alligator Eatery

Since 1995, four of us women go on an annual winter adventure to Oglebay Resort in Wheeling, West Virginia, over the four days of Martin Luther King holiday weekend. Sandie, Martha, Dee, and I drive up Friday leaving at noon. We always pick Oglebay because of the safe, clear, two-hour highway trip in case of potentially bad winter weather—and the resort cabins have cleared paths to them as well. Given the wintry roads and the mountainous conditions of Seven Springs or Hidden Valley, Oglebay is the resort of choice—one that minimizes the anxiety of winter travel.

Sandie, Martha, Dee, and I all met as Carlow University faculty and where Dee remains as an adjunct faculty. Martha and Sandie are retired professors in the Professional Leadership Program. I am a retired director and professor in the Early Childhood Education Program. We began our MLK holiday adventure by going hiking over a long weekend—but we only hiked the first year. We decided to invite Dee. (Dee thought we were inviting her to warn her about some dangerous politicking at Carlow. We were inviting her because we thought she'd be fun—and to warn her of some dangerous politicking at Carlow.)

At 69-years-old, Sandie is a tall woman with short red hair, who is slim, durable, and hearty. She brings the cookies for the ride down and chocolates for the visit. She also grinds the fresh coffee beans and makes coffee each morning. When we've sufficiently awake, she makes oatmeal for breakfast. Sandie has added homemade zucchini soup to our lunch menu. One year, she brought a book of essays about strong women of Seattle—her home town—and read a passage for us. She also brings in the firewood from time to time as we need it.

At 77-years-old, Martha, with spiked brown hair and an impish face, pushes herself to meet challenges—some necessary and some not so necessary. She is retired but has the stress of some serious illnesses. She was diagnosed with Sjörgren's Syndrome, an autoimmune disorder. She also has severe back problems. Three times now, we have taken her from the hospital bed to our retreat. She is a trooper and a good sport, and we are good for her—medicine for her spirit. Martha keeps the fire going all weekend with the firewood from Sandie and does a fine job. Martha brings herself and some wine, and we are honored with her presence.

Dee is 63-years-old, has brown hair with red highlights and is always friendly with a welcoming smile and greeting. Upbeat, cheerful, and positive, she brings an array of foods from homemade beef and noodle soup to the ingredients for a luncheon spinach salad to a bag of oranges. She also carries her tea bags for her daily cups of tea, sharing her tea bags with anyone at will. One year, she did hand massages. She also brings her wonderful sense of humor to the weekend.

I am 68-years-old and the only one with white hair, who is retired and has the stress of health care and living on a fixed income in my life which is a trade-off for when I worked since I was always anxious then too. I make the lunches—sometimes wraps, but, one time, cheeses, breads, and fruit, and, most recently, Mulligatawny Soup. One year, I brought a sketch pad and a set of fine point magic markers for each person. Another year, I brought a coloring book and a box of 96 crayons for each. I like to cultivate the artistic. We are a wonderful, loyal, caring, and compassionate foursome.

Friday at noon we meet, and either Sandie or Dee drives. This year, Dee drove. Our first stop is usually the Subway at the Canonsburg exit on I-79 where we get a half of a sub or salad and begin to wind down. Recently, though, we have met at Dee's house for a wonderful, warm, and pleasant lunch to begin our weekend sojourn. We then proceed to Wheeling, and, on the way, someone writes a list of groceries to buy at the Kroger's. This year, Sandie wrote it on the back of a bank deposit slip. We make a new list every year because it depends on what everyone brings from home.

We have the trip through Kroger's down to an art. In 15 minutes, we can find all of the food as well as fire starters and a lighter. In ten more minutes, we are checked out and on the road climbing up the hill to Wilson Lodge to check in at Oglebay. We always stay in cabins, for they have a rustic charm about them. This year, we upgraded and stayed at Ash Cabin which has four bedrooms and two baths.

Opening the door to a large main room, you will find us lounging on four cushioned chairs, eating cookies and chocolates or sliced apples around the coffee table while talking and enjoying the fire. Against one wall in this main room—covering nearly the whole wall, there is a large stone fireplace with a continuous fire that Martha and I jointly tend. Outside is a sufficient stock of wood with more to be easily obtained by a phone call. Against another wall is a picnic table where you will find us conversing over our oatmeal at breakfast or our zucchini soup with sandwich or salad at lunch.

Around the perimeter of the main room is an assortment of couches, chairs, and end tables with lights for additional congregating or moving to the sidelines to read, write, or nap while still remaining with the group. At different years, the amount of this sideline activity has changed according to our needs—we are flexible and responsive. Martha and Sandie read; I journal; and Dee begins reading but soon ends up napping. On occasion, we each go off to our respective rooms to read and nap. This year, we needed much less private time. Some living rooms have wall paintings, but our cabin has living paintings. As a backdrop to the living room, half a wall of windows look out over the woods in wonderful winter scenes—snow falling and deer running through the trees.

Off of the main room are the four bedrooms going back and two bathrooms in the front. After Sandie's invitation to pick a bedroom, we each select one. Martha and I pick the front two rooms and Sandie and Dee select the back two rooms. We put our clothes away in the wooden chest of drawers and our night clothes on one of the two double-beds in the room. There is a medium window and a rod with a few hangers for a coat and such. It's a simple but functional bedroom. We get situated in a flutter of conversation about how we finally made it to Oglebay—finally!

Off the main room also is a fully equipped kitchen. However, we only use it for coffee and tea, oatmeal in the morning, to make sandwiches or wraps for lunch, and to keep fruit, chocolates, cookies, cheese, and wine for snacks. We go out to dinner every night. Through the years, we've established three places we really like and usually frequent. Friday night, we go to a great hamburger joint, the Alpha, where we continue to unwind for the weekend. Saturday night, we usually go to the Nail Factory, but several years later, we began to go to a crêpe place, Later Alligator. Sunday night, we go to an outstanding Italian eatery, Undo's.

*I take a picture of Martha, Sandie and Dee as we
dine out at Undo's, enjoying the Italian cuisine.*

Our cabin is a respite where we can be with
each other in friendship and caring. We, one and all,
look forward to this adventure every year with eager
anticipation. About seven years ago, we added a
summer retreat in June to Hocking Hills, Ohio—a rural
area about five hours west of Pittsburgh. We like being
together. We anticipate the next retreat as soon as we
conclude the previous one, but when we are immersed
in the experience, there is only being with each of our
friends in the moment.

On Saturday and Sunday, between breakfast and
dinner, we spend a lot of time just talking and laughing
with each other. There is an ebb and flow that fits our
life rhythms of the year—some years we are tired and
some we are energized. Our meals extend for hours
over conversation. Occasionally, we break open a bottle
of wine and talk some more though each of us is only a

one-or-two-glass drinker. We're all on medicine. We talk about Carlow, our lives, romances, life and death, leadership, pets, children, and grandchildren—anything is fuel for discussion. We strive to see the humor in everything that we can.

We have a tradition that we began three years into our visits to Oglebay. We keep a journal for each of us—actually Dee does the recording and keeps the journals. Our mantra is "Write it down; make it happen" from the title of a book by the same name. We each take a turn listening to last year's goals and commentary and giving our own feedback on the progress in each area. Each year, we update our new goals and commentary. This has been an interesting and a wonderful documentation of our individual growth. We are also cheerleaders in hearing each other's progress.

This year, 2014, our personal discussions progressed in a different direction. Because of individual losses that we each faced, we found that we were not so desirous of setting long term goals but of striving to live in the present more—enjoying every moment. The spirit of our weekend together was different. We each and all were embracing the immediate.

Three years ago, in 2010, though, things were different. We drove up in snow to an unpredicted snow storm. Although the roads were fine, we had a challenging weekend ahead without knowing it. However, Sandie did make preparations in case we would not go to the Alpha on Friday for dinner. She brought pesto pasta, which was delicious. We appreciated not having to go outside. I was also having trouble staying awake and stumbling, which I would later find out was a side effect of a new medicine. Sandie, Martha, and Dee were very patient and supportive of me.

Saturday, the electricity went out during the day. We were offered food including warm soup for dinner if we could walk to the Inn to get it. Sandie and Dee trudged through the deep snow to go pick up the food. On the way back, Sandie slipped on some ice, fell, and hurt herself. However, being somewhat hearty women, we ate and settled in for the night, but the wood was so green that we could not enjoy what should have been the ongoing heat and fire in the fireplace.

The Inn offered us lodging for the night because they had electricity, but we initially refused. We wanted to have our own space. However, after several cold hours and several calls from the Inn, we agreed and packed up for the night. In the Inn, I fell backward and hit my head on the floor of the main stairwell to our rooms. I roomed with Dee, and Sandie and Martha roomed together. The next morning, over breakfast in the Inn restaurant, we noted how we had all gone immediately to sleep in psychic exhaustion.

By this time, we were ready to go home a day and a half early—the Inn was not for us. The clerk informed us that the electricity was back on in the cabin, but it was too late. We went home. We had had enough.

We drove home and still had to dig out of 2 ½ feet of snow. We started out with the pasta to cope with the weather, but the weather got too overwhelming. We would all return home to a comfortable environment. We did not even make our usual reservation for the following year. Nevertheless, as we talked over 2011, we decided we'd give Oglebay a try again in 2012 but with a newer cabin and a warning about the green wood. Life was like this with a combination of comfort and challenges. We dealt with both.

Winter 2012 was a wonderful visit to Oglebay. We had great fires all day long to keep us warm and set the scene. Martha and I jointly tended the fire even though each of us had back problems. The wood was perfect for burning.

We ate healthy food. At the Alpha, we all forewent our burgers and had broiled fish dinners. For breakfasts, we had oatmeal. For lunch, we had spinach salads with carrots, chick peas, green beans, and organic cranberries. Instead of the Nail Factory, we decided to try a new crêpe place, Later Alligator, which was a fun change. For all our dinners out, we showed restraint. We snacked on oranges and apples although we did allow ourselves the luxury of chocolates, cookies, and brownies.

The group invited me to bring my life story writings and read them aloud. They were very enthusiastic about my works. I read two or three each day to wonderful, supportive comments and encouragement. The verbal photographs I wrote of Sandie, Martha, and Dee were kept in our "write it down; make it happen" journal. I was to send them an email with their individual copies of their stories. I felt thrilled by all of this.

With the support and empathy of good friends, we talked about different family matters that were on our minds. We are very good at being listeners and sounding boards who are also responsive. However, we do not react any differently toward these family members after hearing the stories. We were inclusive as we welcomed Sandie's family to celebrate her granddaughter's birthday with us Saturday afternoon.

Sunday night the fire went out to conclude the weekend, and Monday morning's breakfast at Perkins Pancake House provided the transition back to the work-a-day world. The weekend was a restorative interlude. We felt revived and well loved—nourished and nurtured. We knew the camaraderie of strong friendships. We were ready for the upcoming challenges ahead of us—and eagerly await our next retreat in June.

A Spunky Woman: Martha

*Martha has a positive attitude
and tremendous strength of will.
She is one hell of a woman.*

Although an introvert by nature, Martha is one of the most socially skilled and well-liked people I know. People seek out her company.

Martha is an enigma, a woman of contrasts. She is an intellectual and a jock. She reads heavy duty, theoretical texts and psychological mysteries. She is quite successful socially but an introvert at heart. She is always kind—listening carefully to others and encouraging their ideas. She can be most charming in conversation and yet sometimes argumentative—maybe because of her rhetorical background. But whatever the aspect of Martha that is showing, she draws people to her with her magnetic personality. People want to talk to her about professional leadership or themselves, sit by her, and generally bask in her attention.

Martha has risen to the many challenges in her life.

Martha taught with a passion for communications and professional leadership. She was a beloved mentor, assigned formally or chosen informally, to a number of the teaching staff at Carlow. In teaching, she kept *au courant* with technology, current teaching strategies, and content and cemented good work relationships with the students. Martha was an outstanding teacher, and her students adored her. In fact, everyone at Carlow was very fond of her. When she retired from Carlow, she was named Professor Emerita for her years of outstanding teaching, service, and scholarship. The faculty gave her a standing ovation.

Martha is a seventy-seven-year-old woman, who is 5'2" with an impish smile and short, mostly brown, spiked hair. She wears sports clothes often topped by the sweatshirts or jackets of her grandchildren hailing from Dartmouth, Marquette, the University of Wisconsin, and St. Louis University. For quite a few years, Martha, Sandie, and I taught at Carlow and lived in Shadyside, an upper middle class community in the city of Pittsburgh. During some of this time, Martha was finishing up her doctoral dissertation. For a while, when Sandie and I walked with her around Shadyside on Sunday mornings, we both strongly encouraged Martha to "Get your dissertation done. It is on health care and so timely." Eventually, she overcame the travails of doctoral studies.

Although some might say Martha was a workaholic, she really did know how to relax around her friends. When I was teaching with Martha for many years, we ate dinner at Max and Erma's on Walnut Street in Shadyside on Friday nights. We would discuss any and all things from Carlow and teaching to men. We had serious conversations punctuated by stories and laughter. Often, Martha was willing to share her huge cut of banana cream pie with me. On occasion, Sandie joined us, but Martha and I were regulars for this delightful Friday evening ritual.

Sandie (front) joins Martha and me one Friday evening for our Friday ritual dinner.

Then the trials of illness entered Martha's life. She had back surgery first. Soon after, she moved from a third floor walk-up in Shadyside to a first floor apartment in the North Hills near her daughter. Now, I eagerly await her morning phone calls to keep in touch. I look forward to our talking about retirement, health issues, life story writing, her grandchildren, our cats, and life in general. Talking for more than an hour, I find the conversations to be stimulating and invigorating—and funny. She does have a wonderful sense of humor, and we laugh at how ironic life can be.

Then, Martha got sick with an autoimmune disease, Sjörgren's Syndrome. But she has been a fighter over the years. She continued to teach as long as she could even through great discomfort. She will go out to dinner every chance she gets if that is at all possible—sometimes she is vulnerable to picking up viruses and infections and thus cannot go out. Recently, she received a few doses of chemotherapy. They worked. Martha's illness was less consuming. We—her family and her good friends—celebrated.

And we continue to talk on the phone often—nearly every morning.

It makes me sad to see my friend, Martha, suffering from this terrible disease. And it makes me angry. I miss hanging out with my friend. But she is a fighter. Martha even joined us again—Sandie, Dee, and me—at Oglebay for our four-day weekend in January. The four of us have done this since 1995 and for nearly 20 years. We have even rescued her from a hospital bed three times to take her with us to our cabin retreat. She does not give up or give in. She is feisty and courageous.

Kudos to Martha!

Healthy Meal: Fast Turkey Chili

Martha's hearty, tasty chili has fortified us at Oglebay and been the hit at parties. The turkey meat makes this chili lighter and less fatty than beef chili, but it still has plenty of flavor.

Ingredients:
1 t vegetable oil
1 medium red bell pepper, diced into ½" pieces
1 medium onion, chopped
1 medium green bell pepper, diced
2 celery stalks, thinly sliced
1 lb. ground turkey
4 minced garlic cloves
28-oz. can crushed tomatoes
¼ c. mild chili powder
14.5-oz. can crushed tomatoes
15-oz. can pinto beans, drained
9-oz. box frozen corn
1 t dried oregano
salt to taste

Directions:
Heat a large pot over high heat. Add oil, spreading it so it evenly coats the bottom of the pot.

When the oil is hot, add the onion, peppers, celery, and turkey meat. Cook, stirring often, until turkey is done, about 2 minutes.

Add garlic and cook 1 more minute.

Add chili powder, and cook continuously for another minute.

Add tomatoes, beans, oregano, and salt. Stir.

Bring the chili to a boil, then reduce the heat to low and simmer, partially covered, for 20 minutes, stirring occasionally.

Add frozen corn and stir to combine. Cook 10 more minutes.

Yield: 6 1¼-cup servings

Camaraderie: Sandie

Sandie is always ready to discuss a topic, collaborate or brainstorm an idea.

I earned two weeks of free pasta dinners in exchange for creating seven menus—both printing the inside text and painting the outside cover—for an Italian eatery in London while I was living there for three months on a tight budget. Pasta was economical and nutritious— especially with whole grain noodles. It was a wonderful way to get an inexpensive, filling meal that was healthy. I love pasta to this day. Sandie, my colleague from Carlow University and my good friend, introduced me to my first simple, make-it-yourself tomato sauce recipe.

Sandie and I became friends over 20 years ago in 1993 when we began a tradition of walking through Shadyside every Saturday morning. We get coffee at Jitters, a local, privately-owned coffee house. Its clientele features a range of ages of people who are also mainly upper-middle class patrons. Sandie and I started the weekend walk followed by coffee at Jitters when I was living in Shadyside and when she had just moved to Pittsburgh. I continue to walk in Shadyside because I enjoy the opportunity to be in my old neighborhood. We walk all year around.

Our walk is between one and three miles a day depending on me. Sandie is tall and hearty and walks faster than me, a shorter, less vigorous walker. She accommodates my pace, and we have wonderful conversations while we walk. Always listening carefully to each other, we first take turns reporting about the week's happenings. Speaking with heart and liveliness, we once discussed teaching and shared our insights. Talking about teaching had been a paramount topic of discussion. Before we retired, we would brainstorm each other's teaching dilemmas. Now, I listen to her discussion of a few, occasional school issues since she continues some very part-time work at Carlow in her retirement and she hears my stories of my facilitating a life story writing group. We share reflections and observations. I also am working with master's level students on theses, and Sandie contributes insights on working with these students and their documents. Sandie is a wonderful collaborator. I learn so much as we immerse ourselves in discussions—about teaching, relating, and life in general.

Sandie is also great at brainstorming about anything. So, for example, when I expressed, "I want to do art in hospice with children and adolescents who have experienced a loss, but schlepping things around is a turn off," Sandie responded, "I can help you think through that. I think you should get a polka dot backpack or a suitcase on wheels." Then we talked further about leak proof paint containers. She's always full of ideas.

Sandie and I continue our conversation at Jitters over cappuccino for her and a diet Coke for me. I am hot from the walk. We spent many months, for example, talking about our mutual friend, Martha, and how we could be a supportive friend to her during her debilitating disease and its return. Amazingly, even though she did not have cancer, the chemo worked against her autoimmune disease, and she is now less bothered by it.

And, of course, we always have our proprietary discussions about men.

Retirement is sometimes on our minds. We talk about my retirement and the specific Osher courses in flash fiction and creative writing that I have taken, as well as my participating in a life story writing group. Sandie is very encouraging about my taking courses and my writing and calls me her "role model for retirement." I retired a year earlier than I planned and had no idea what I would do. I found my way to Osher and the life story writing group. Sometimes, Sandie converses about her own retirement. We are good supports for one another.

With my retirement, I have come to love cooking. Cooking is an occasional topic of conversation too. She has given me a wonderful recipe for zucchini soup which I love—the same soup she brings to our retreats with Martha and Dee. She also introduced me to a recipe for simply-made, delicious tomato sauce for pasta or lasagna. With retirement, I need to be economical and yet eat healthily, so her soup and sauce are perfect. These recipes contribute to my repertoire of scrumptious foods to make.

Zucchini Soup

Ingredients:
1 large onion, chopped
2 T oil or butter
3 8" zucchini, sliced and unpeeled
5 c. water
5 chicken bouillon cubes

Directions:
Sauté onion in oil or butter. Cook until onions are soft.

In another pot, add zucchini to water and bouillon. Bring water to a boil and then reduce heat and simmer until zucchini is soft.

Pour onion mixture into broth and zucchini mixture.

Purée in blender.

Serve hot or cold.

Italian Tomato Sauce

Ingredients:
3 T olive oil
1 c. onion, chopped
1 T minced garlic
2 t basil
1 c. green pepper, chopped
½ lb. mushrooms, coarsely chopped (optional)
1 t oregano
2 bay leaves
2 t salt
1 1 lb.-13 oz can tomato puree
1 6-oz can tomato paste
2 T dry red wine
1 c. tomatoes, freshly chopped
¼ t black pepper
½ c. parsley, freshly chopped
½ c. grated parmesan or Romano (optional)

Directions:
Sautée onion, garlic, basil, green pepper, mushrooms (optional), oregano, bay leaves, and salt in olive oil until onions are clear and very soft.

Add tomato purée, tomato paste, red wine, chopped tomatoes, and black pepper. Reduce to low heat. Cover pot and simmer at least 45 minutes, stirring occasionally.

Add parsley and salt and pepper to taste.

Top with parmesan or Romano, if desired.

Radical Hospitality: Dee

*Dee welcomes her numerous friends
on First Wednesdays—
and all days.*

Dee smiles and laughs easily.

Dee is a psychotherapist, a consultant, and an adjunct faculty at Carlow University. Her consulting focuses on professional leadership and development. As adjunct faculty, she teaches leadership courses often for the School of Nursing. She is self-employed and works long and hard hours, often 12-hour days. Dee loves her work—and she loves to work. But she also loves to cook and entertain in her home.

Dee leaves the main door of her house open, welcoming all to First Wednesday as she cooks dinner in the kitchen. She had a wonderful role model in her mother. When Dee was growing up, dinner was always opened to anyone who dropped by, with room for another chair or two or three to squeeze at the table.

Beginning in 2001 and continuing for eight years, Dee hosted First Wednesday at her house on the first Wednesday of every month during the academic year. A week or so ahead of the event, a postcard came in the mail to remind each of us of the dinner and give directions to her house on the North Side of Pittsburgh. Her home, built during the Depression, had two floors with a wonderful stairway in the center of the living room and kitchen and was open to all of her friends. Thirty to 40 people visited her on any given First Wednesday.

The glow of lit candles was interspersed throughout the house, and wonderful aromas of chicken tortilla soup, spaghetti and meatballs, and pumpkin and curry soup greeted each guest as they entered. Off to one side, Rosemarie could be heard having joyful conversation on Martin Seligman's books on positive psychology and books on professional leadership with Barbara and Hetz. In another corner, Sandie, Martha, and Roberta were having a conversation mixed with laughter and tenderness over the foibles of the faculty at Carlow University, their mutual employer.

In the living room, lit candles in the fireplace, like a fire of candles, lent warmth to the room. Cheeses from the Strip District's Pennsylvania Macaroni Company accompanied crackers on the coffee table as appetizers to stave off the hunger of the guests—and created an atmosphere for people's congregating and conversing with each other as they arrived. We talked about everything from the TV show, Gray's Anatomy, to Hillary and Obama's first run for the presidential nomination. From 4:00 PM when friends began to arrive, people dropped in or stayed till 9:00 PM or so when the last guests departed.

Dee was in the kitchen preparing a main meal like spinach soufflé, and she always had a delicious loaf of bread sliced from Enrico's in the Strip District. Often, there would be a green, leafy salad too. She had wine, beer and soft drinks. Her friends were invited to come with a dish or bottle of wine—or simply come as they were. People brought foods such as huge, homemade, chocolate-covered strawberries, warmed brie cheese, cut up fresh vegetables, home-baked ginger cookies, sweet pea and basil soup, banana bread, vegetarian casserole, and chocolate cake. Nothing was organized *per se*, but there was always an abundance of food and beverage. It was easy for each of us to relate to one another in conversation—after all, we had the friendship of Dee in common.

Some friends congregated in the kitchen with Dee, who wore bright reds, purples, or dramatic blacks, one of a collection of cheap wrist watches which she was very proud to own, and dangling earrings. Friends talked and laughed with her over a glass of wine as she cooked, and we shared in Dee's joy with life. Dee's presence was infectious as we were lifted up by her positive energy toward life and people. She always looks for the positive in everyone—and she found it.

Dee welcomed Sharon to her home, introducing her by saying, "Here is Sharon, a visiting professor from China. She is doing research on American higher education at the University of Pittsburgh." Also, she said, for example, "Ellen, can I tell everybody about your writings? And what Osher

138

courses are you taking this term? Ellen is our role model for retirement."

Others met on the enclosed porch warmed by a wood-burning stove in the winter. Still others visited with each other in the dining room around the table with an artistically designed, different, patterned plate for each place setting. Although all were close to Dee, this was radical hospitality. Included were her children and stepchildren, her former dates, her friends from Carlow, her friends from other jobs, her church friends, and so many more. All were welcome and included. Dee modeled this—as her mother once had—and shared her home, her warmth, and her friends with each other. We are fortunate to have Dee and to have had this monthly event as a part of our lives. While First Wednesday has ended, we continue to be inspired by this model of radical hospitality—our friend, Dee. Dee had hoped that someone else might pick up the notion of First Wednesday, but we all knew that none of us could do it. Dee did First Wednesday masterfully.

Spinach Soufflé

Dee served this soufflé at one of her many First Wednesday dinners.

Ingredients:
1 bunch spinach, washed with stems removed
1 small onion, grated
3 T butter
3 c. flour
¾ c. milk
1 pinch nutmeg
salt
pepper
4 egg yolks
7 egg whites
parmesan cheese

Directions:
Preheat oven to 375.

Blanche spinach 4-5 minutes using only water clinging to the leaves. Drain well and rinse in cold water. Dry thoroughly and chop coarsely.

Melt butter in saucepan. Add onion. Cook, without browning, until very soft.

Remove from heat. Stir in flour. Gradually blend in milk. Season. Add spinach.

Blend in blender until thoroughly mixed.

Pour into large bowl. Beat in egg yolks.

Beat egg whites until stiff, but not dry. Gently fold into spinach base.

Pour into a greased, medium casserole dish. Sprinkle lightly with cheese.

Bake 17-20 minutes or until well-risen, puffed, and nicely browned.

Serve immediately.

Soups: Me

I enjoy cooking and eating all kinds of soups at all times of year.

Beef and chicken soup, split pea soup, beef and barley soup, chicken soup—they were the only soups I knew how to make, and I cooked chicken soup often.

Then I met Al Kosmal. He is a charming and knowledgeable chef, who has a wonderful sense of humor. He also is a terrific cook and instructor for the cooking courses in my Osher Life Long Learning classes at the University of Pittsburgh. Soups, Soups and More Soups introduced me to Al. In the first class that I attended at Pitt Osher, I learned about, and got recipes for, ten new soups that I had never previously made. Since retirement, I became hooked on cooking, and this was one more opportunity to enjoy myself. Over the years, cooking and consuming soups was always a favorite past time of mine. Soups nourish the body and the soul; they sooth me too.

In fact, my best friend, Janet, who shares my cooking interest, further nurtured my passion for it by sending me the book of recipes, *Soups, Chowders, Consommés, and Broths: Over 200 Inspirational Recipes from around the World*, to allow me to create even more soups, many with a cross cultural flavor. A Moroccan harira soup, cooked with lamb, vegetables, lentils, and chick peas, was used for Ramadan and was my first new addition to my repertoire. After that recipe, I added a mulligatawny soup, a chicken curry soup with vegetables, fruit, and lentils brought to England from India. Likewise, I chose English cock-a-leekie, a kind of chicken soup with leeks. Soups became a theme of my cooking all year around, but especially in the winter months.

During the 2012 fall semester, Al offered a class in Healthy Eating, which I enrolled in, and we enjoyed Cucumber Soup. In the 2013 spring semester, he taught a course, Soups and Salads, which I attended. I am trying to cook interesting, tasty, and also healthy meals. He approved of this hearty Mulligatawny Soup, which warmed us at Oglebay.

Mulligatawny Soup

Ingredients:
4 T butter or oil
2 large chicken breasts with skin on and bones in
1 onion, chopped
1 carrot, chopped
1 small turnip, chopped
1 T curry powder
4 cloves
6 black peppercorns, lightly crushed
¼ c. lentils
4 c. chicken stock
¼ c. yellow raisins
salt and pepper to taste

Directions:
Melt butter or heat oil in a large sauce pan, then brown the chicken over a brisk heat. Transfer browned chicken onto a plate and set aside.

Add onion, carrots, and turnips to the pan and cook, stirring occasionally until lightly colored. Stir in curry powder, cloves, and peppercorns. Cook for 1-2 minutes, then add lentils.

Pour the stock into the pot. Bring to a boil. Add raisins, chicken, and any juices from the plate. Cover and simmer gently for 1 ¼ hours.

Remove the chicken from the pot and allow to cool.

Discard the skin and bones. Cut into pieces, return to pot.

Reheat before serving.

Yield: 4 servings

Recipes from Piccolo Forno

Friends over forty-some years, Karen, Rosemarie, Roberta, and I gather for lunch, monthly, usually on a Friday. Our friendships are rooted in the 1970s at the University of Pittsburgh Program in Child Development/ Child Care. Rosemarie, Roberta, and I were advanced degree students, and Karen was one of the faculty in the Program. We've maintained a friendship over the years. We have our own little community of four that meets at Piccolo Forno eatery in the Lawrenceville section of Pittsburgh, Pennsylvania. The restaurant serves a range of Tuscan cuisine—always fresh, homemade, and delicious. The chef's area is enclosed in glass so that you can see him or her working using a wood-burning fire.

We can be high powered women, but we also can be in touch with our softer side.

Roberta has been Dean of the School of Education, taught on overload, consulted with child care agencies and with Fred Rogers, and been vice president for the National Association for the Education of Young Children. Rosemarie has held the position of administrator at Western Psychiatric Institute and Clinic (WPIC), a nationally recognized excellent center for psychiatric care. She currently has her own business as a job coach, consultant, and psychotherapist. Karen has a long affiliation at the University of Pittsburgh, a research 1 university; has published extensively; and is a consultant. Yet we are all nurturers. Janice is our newest member of the group and an entrepreneur.

Over lunch, we have impassioned discussions of the books we are currently reading. We have conversed about writings of Hillary Clinton, Brené Brown, Barbara Fredrickson, and Martin Seligman. We also examine attachment issues and bullying, relationship concerns such as shame and vulnerability, the 2012 national election and racism, and current issues in child development and child care. Roberta and Rosemarie also share joyful stories about their grandchildren to a receptive audience.

We gather around the scrumptious food which nourishes us and fuels our conversation. Karen loves the eggplant meal; Roberta enjoys the polenta dish; and I savor the tuna and cannellini bean salad. We all enthusiastically share our plates of food with the others. The portions are generous, so Rosemarie, who often joins us a little later because she is coming from a client, shares our meals or dessert afterward. Janice has begun to join our group when she can and enjoys the hearty, homemade soups. The wait staff is young, friendly, and efficient—our wait person even remembers, from month to month, that I don't like raw onions on my salad.

We all have begun to share personal writings with each other as one more way to enjoy camaraderie and community. We take turns reading our works, and all participate in a lively discussion of the writings including giving positive, encouraging feedback. In fact, because we encouraged Rosemarie, she submitted her story, Philomena's Christmas Eve Pasta, to the *Pittsburgh Post-Gazette*, and it was published. We are an enthusiastic writing audience and support group for each other.

I have listed the four members of our group in the order of length of time that I have known each of them. The recipes included here are ones that each person chose.

- **Roberta's Whole Wheat Buns** are a treat for family and friends especially on cold days.

- **Rosemarie's** rendition of **Philomena's Christmas Eve Pasta** is a delicious family recipe that all of us have tried and savored.

- **Karen's Ice Shakes** cleverly provide for a creamy diet shake.

- **Janice's Bourbon Balls** are a festive delight.

- **My Curried Turkey Wrap** nourishes the dieter as well as the non-dieter.

Miles to Go: Roberta

Roberta is at home in the city or on a farm—and always the loved wife, mother and grandmother and cherished child development professional.

Roberta and I jogged an impressive 3.2 miles each day, five days a week, for two years, no matter what the weather. We had known each other since graduate school in the early 1970s. Soon after we met, I moved to Morningside where she lived, and we began jogging. She had a family, so she called me at 6:30 AM. No one was awakened by the ringing of the phone since I lived alone. We met about three minutes into our run and jogged together down the side streets of Morningside out to Negley Avenue. At Negley, we turned left and continued on Negley to the Highland Park Reservoir. We ran around the reservoir two times and then returned the same route back home by 7:05 AM.

I then showered and went to work, and Roberta had coffee and read the paper for a half an hour before her family got up—a treasured time for her until, soon, the family started to wake up at 7:05 AM too. We jogged at a comfortable pace to enable us to talk. We quit after Roberta was so far along in her pregnancy with twins that jogging became impossible. I was disappointed. I dearly missed our time together. She gave birth to two delightful boys.

During those two years of jogging before the twin boys arrived, we talked a lot. We conversed about our dreams by night, adventures by day, but especially our studies by semester. A small study group of two, we discussed American higher education in preparation for our comprehensive exams. We examined topics such as academic freedom, the history of institutions of higher education, the structure of the institution, and so on.

Additionally, one summer, we added a personal challenge to the mix. Roberta wanted to lose ten pounds by August. I wanted to quit smoking. So we agreed to put away $25.00 each to save. We would have a contest. Every day for 25 days, we already had a dollar in the pot. On the 26th day and so forth, we would each add a dollar to our respective pots. By vacation time in August, we would each have $90.00 if we kept our part of the challenge—Roberta would have to lose ten pounds, and I would have to continue to quit smoking. But if one of us failed in the challenge, the other one got all of the money. Ninety dollars was a nice sum of money in the 1970s, but $180.00 was very impressive.

So, when we were jogging, and Roberta said, "I was tempted by a piece of cherry pie last night after dinner," I good-naturedly joked, "Oh, Roberta, you should eat the pie!"

When I told her, "I really wanted a cigarette when we had coffee after dinner," she teasingly encouraged me, "Ellen, you should have a cigarette!"

This bantering continued, but neither of us ever gave in. In August, Roberta had $90.00 to spend on her vacation in California, and I had $90.00 to buy magnifying lenses for my single lens reflex camera. I took it with me to Florida for my visit to the botanical gardens in Miami. Roberta and I had fun and had successfully saved some money—a profitable endeavor.

During our two years of jogging, we also co-consulted for Title XX Day Care for Pennsylvania, 20 hours a week. At this time, we traveled to various sites in southwestern Pennsylvania from Indiana to New Castle in order to facilitate and teach good practices in child development: the use of the arts and of play for self-expression with young children; psychosocial development and learning; and the support of effective behavior development and self-regulation.

The child care personnel in various day care agencies constantly called us to return for additional training. We designed the training proposals to receive the contracts and designed the educational materials. We were quite a duo, and I loved our work together. Often, we talked about our consulting during our jogging adventures. After Roberta's family went to sleep at 10:00 PM or so, we followed up the early morning discussion with late evening development of proposals and educational materials for an hour or two. Roberta is a remarkable person, who could fit this all in her life—still can. Our friendship grew, developed, and flourished during these two years of daily jogging.

I feel very fortunate to have Roberta as a friend still today. In fact, we have co-consulted after a fashion—she was first reader and I was second reader on many master's thesis documents in early childhood education at Carlow University. Although the distant location of our homes from each other does not permit us to walk every day—she lives in Cranberry Township to the north of Pittsburgh, and I live in Monroeville to the east—we have continued to enjoy working together thanks to computers. Neither of us could jog anymore. Thankfully, we do have our monthly lunches as a foursome at Piccolo Forno to keep in touch.

Roberta is a nurturing person. Once, when we were on our way to consult for Title XX Day Care, she was concerned that I wasn't eating adequately. Roberta bought me a dinner without making a fuss. She made me feel cared for. One way that Roberta nurtures is through cooking. She is a wonderful cook and baker. In fact, I email her from time to time to inquire about recipes when I am cooking. Also, over the years, she has treated me to a number of delicious, homemade foods at her home. One of her specialties is homemade breads. The aroma of the homemade bread tantalizes me as I enter her house and whets my appetite for the bread soon to follow. Since I am a novice at bread baking, she has shared her simplest of bread recipes with me.

Roberta's Whole Wheat Buns

This recipe has been adapted from the *Deaf Smith County Cookbook*.

Ingredients:
2 T dry yeast
1 c. lukewarm water
1 cup hot water
1/3 cup honey (If you are using one measuring cup, measure the oil first and then honey will slide out)
¾ cup oil (walnut gives it a nutty taste)
2 tsp. sea salt (I often omit this)
2 eggs, beaten
6 c. whole wheat flour (Roberta sometimes mixes ½ whole wheat and ½ unbleached.)

Directions:
Mix yeast and lukewarm water and set aside.

Mix hot water, honey, oil, and salt together well. Then add eggs and the yeast mixture.

Gradually add whole wheat flour.

Mix well in between additions of flour

If to be used immediately, add a little more flour.

Roberta usually let it sit for a couple of hours—but not more than 2 hours—in a cool place and came back to it. She had four kids underfoot when she baked these every week. The dough is easier to mold when chilled anyway.

Divide mixture in half and roll out on a large bread board (or cutting board) until ½" to ¾" inch thick. Cut with biscuit cutter or other round cutter. Bake on an oiled cookie sheet for 10-15 minutes at 400 degrees.

Watch carefully and remove when done.

Feeding the Soul: Rosemarie

*Rosemarie—a nurturer in her personal and
professional life but also with the soul of a poet*

When Rosemarie walks into a room, she is striking to
look at with her blond, short feathered hair, deep
brown eyes, and tawny complexion. She is lively and
humorous as she tells stories of the day's events,
improving them with her sense of drama and
storytelling. She is a passionate Italian, who speaks with
an animated face and hand gestures as she tells a story.
But to me, Rosemarie is a nurturer most of all.

Her new home is a charming, gutted-out home
on Penn Avenue in Lawrenceville, artistically and
creatively done with the kitchen as the hub.
Conversations arise in the kitchen as she prepares a
dinner for her guests who sit at stools at the island. She

tosses salad or mixes pasta with sauce as we converse. Rosemarie loves to cook, and she lovingly cooks. On a number of occasions, she has had me to her house for meals. Although I know that the food was delicious—it always is—her way of making me feel cared for was more important.

The second hub in her house is the dining room where we all meet to enjoy the delicious, lovingly-prepared, home-cooked meal. Hours are spent around the dining room table, eating sumptuous food, sharing in good talk, telling lively stories, and drinking wine. Laughter and good cheer abound. One evening, six of us, including Rosemarie and me, had a dinner to honor our mentor from the 70s, Ellie. At Rosemarie's suggestion, we told stories of how Ellie influenced each of us over wine and a dinner of pasta in a homemade red pasta sauce with pine nuts and raisins, a roasted chicken, and salad. The stories were a wonderful addition, and Ellie was moved by them.

In former days, Rosemarie and I nurtured ourselves with our occasional visits to the opera. At Amoré, an upscale restaurant in Oakland, we enjoyed a delicious meal, good wine, and convivial conversation. We dressed to the nines for this event. Listening to Puccini or Mozart, for example, we delighted in the beauty of the music, costume, and song—and nurtured our souls.

Sister Rita Alice was a faculty member at Carlow University, whom both Rosemarie and I knew well. She was Rosemarie's competent, compassionate, and gifted advisor and instructor in speech pathology, Rosemarie's major. She was my caring and knowledgeable colleague on the faculty of Carlow University. The three of us met for lunch at the convent from time to time to enjoy good conversation and laughter. Sister Rita Alice, too, had quite a sense of humor and was a good storyteller.

Rosemarie is a psychotherapist and a job coach by trade. She nurtures in her career. She is one of the most positive people I know, always looking for the strengths in people. She believes in—and lives—positivist psychology. Inherent in this discipline is the focus on what's right with a person rather than what's wrong. She is life affirming. She focuses on resilience. Once when I was hospitalized and she was the administrator for my unit, she visited me as a friend and had me call her at home when I needed to hear a friendly voice. She invited me to her house for meals when I was discharged.

In between all of my hospitalizations, she would call and try to take me out to window shop or go to lunch. She put the energy into maintaining this friendship when I was at a low ebb in my life and could not be very reciprocal. I was so depressed that I cannot even recall the specifics of all that she did for me, but, I know that, during this very difficult time, she was caring and supportive. She never abandoned me even though I was very depressed and not very responsive. She also conveyed that there was life after being hospitalized. I don't know that she has given me the opportunity to be as reciprocal to her when she needed support or encouragement, although I hope to do so in the future.

Over the years, I have come to know Rosemarie and enjoy her friendship. Her wonderful sense of humor during her storytelling keeps me laughing—something good for the soul. She is also inclusive and welcomes all to her gatherings. Recently, she worked toward bringing a friend of hers, Janice, and me together after not seeing each other in many years. Janice and I team-taught forty years ago but had lost touch with each other over the last two decades. Rosemarie and I discovered that we both knew Janice, and that she is one of Rosemarie's friends from Lawrenceville. I look forward to one more opportunity to be with Rosemarie and a friend in camaraderie. We now also include Janice in our Piccolo Forno lunches.

Philomena's Christmas Eve Pasta

Rosemarie has included this recipe of her grandmother, Philomena, who "infuses love into the dish"—a main ingredient in Rosemarie's cooking too. In fact, Rosemarie infuses love in all that she has done for me—and all that she does.

Ingredients:
2 tablespoons olive oil
1 can anchovies,[1] chopped
2 large cloves garlic, chopped
2 1-lb. cans Italian tomatoes in puree
1 can chopped tomatoes or whole tomatoes
½ c. pine nuts, roasted until light brown in a small skillet
1 c. raisins
1 can medium pitted olives, sliced
1 lb. cappellini pasta (angel hair)
parmesan or Romano cheese (optional)

Directions:
Heat olive oil in a large skillet or pot. Add oil from can of anchovies. Chop anchovies into small, ¼" slices. Add slices to pot and heat on medium for about 3 minutes. Anchovies should start to melt. Add chopped

---

[1] Don't allow anchovies to intimidate you. The anchovies disintegrate into the oil and all that's left is a delicious (and important to the integrity of this pasta!), subtle, earthy taste. I have served this to those who say they do not like anchovies, and they have loved it.

garlic. Cook three minutes longer or until garlic bubbles.

Prepare whole tomatoes by pouring into a bowl and squishing them with your hands, breaking up the clumps of tomato into small pieces. Add this sauce and the puree to the pot. Cook for ten minutes, stirring occasionally.

Add roasted pine nuts and raisins. You can add pepper for taste, if you wish. Cook 20 minutes longer.

Add sliced olives. Cook sauce 5 more minutes. Do not overcook sauce as the olives will discolor the it.

Cook pasta in 4 quarts of salted, boiling water following the pasta box directions—usually 4-5 minutes (or until al dente). Drain pasta.

Place 1/3 of sauce into a large, wide pasta serving dish (or you can use individual serving plates if you mix the pasta and sauce in a large pot). Add pasta and slowly turn with a pasta server fork to integrate sauce into pasta. Keep adding sauce and turning until all pasta is coated with sauce. Cappellini absorbs sauce, so it may take a few minutes to mix the sauce and pasta together. Top with parmesan or Romano if you prefer.

Buon Appetitio!

Yield: Plenty

A Fun, Type-A Friend: Karen

In retirement, Karen is honing her creative writing skills while continuing to do scholarly work.

Karen is a Renaissance woman. She has published over 400 scholarly publications. Affiliated with the University of Pittsburgh for over 50 years, Karen was a student and then an esteemed faculty member in the Department of Applied Psychology in the School of Education. I met her during my doctoral studies when she was on the faculty of what was then called the Department of Child Development and Child Care in the School of Health Related Professions. I loved that program, which was rich in intellectual stimulation and challenge. As a valued faculty member, Karen was a part of the scholarly faculty that nurtured and supported applied research. She especially taught curriculum, children's play, and professional writing courses. In 2011, she retired as Professor Emerita and leaves an impressive legacy at the University of Pittsburgh.

Karen can be a jock as well. She loves scuba diving and goes every chance she can. She travels to places like Florida, the Bahamas, and the Caribbean. She collects and shows beautiful shells. Karen has also been known to pick up a game of basketball at the Jewish Community Center. She swims frequently in the summer at the Highland Park City of Pittsburgh pool. Likewise, she can be found walking or riding her bike around her neighborhood in Squirrel Hill. In her 70s, Karen inspires me to keep physically fit as I am aging.

Karen knows a lot about a lot. She carries on conversations about fractals, pencil sketching, politics, creative writings, chaos theory, and more. We have lunches once a month at a variety of places sometimes in Oakland—the Middle Eastern cuisine at Ali Baba or an eclectic menu at the University Club. Traveling to Lawrenceville, we may enjoy the Tuscan food at Piccolo Forno. Lately, we have been coming to Taipei Tokyo in Monroeville for Chinese and sushi. Karen enjoys saki—raw salmon on sushi rice which she likes with ginger, wasabi, and spicy mayonnaise. She says, "It tastes like the sea and a fresh ocean wind." Karen also delights in avocado and salmon rolls. I enjoy miso soup and California rolls with wasabi whose spice makes my nose and my eyes water. We both enjoy eating.

But the best part of our lunches is the friendship shared through conversation. We talk about everything from intellectual endeavors to politics to personal dilemmas. Karen may talk about her book expanding Erik Erikson's stages of adult development, and I may talk about my Osher Life Long Learning classes on Bob Dylan, American Political Fiction and Stories and Mythology. Discussing books we've just read is a part of our lunches too. We also have some good laughs together as we see the humor and irony in the foibles of life.

Lately we have also included a new dimension of self-disclosure—reading and discussing memoirs that we have written about our childhood—from outdoor play to girlish dresses to dance class. Memoirs from our adulthood have been recently added to our repertoire. During one recent luncheon, we read writings on the drudgeries of house cleaning and the frustration of weight control. We both hate to clean and like to eat. Karen has quite a collection of writings, and they demonstrate impressive writing skill and memory recall especially from her childhood. Through our personal writings, we are getting to know each other better and better—and that is a joyful event.

Karen's Ice Shakes

Everybody wants their cold shakes to be creamy—but how to do it without heavy cream increasing the calorie count? Here's Karen's self-designed recipe for a strawberry "ice shake":

Ingredients:
1-1½ c. ice cubes
½ c. 1 or 2 % milk
½ c. powdered non-fat dairy creamer (this is the secret ingredient)
1-2 T strawberry jam
several ripe strawberries (optional)
½ packet Sweet and Low
1 t vanilla

Directions:
Place ingredients in a blender, putting in the ice cubes first and allowing them to begin to melt while you prepare the other ingredients. Blend at high speed until smooth, thick, and creamy.

Pour into a large glass or mug with a handle.

Twenty Years, but Who's Counting?: Janice D.

Happily, I find Janice D. doing well and living in Lawrenceville.

She entered carrying two, small, delicate yellow tulips, snipped with a stem about eight inches long and with one leaf firmly holding on. Although I hadn't seen her in over 20 years, I recognized her engaging smile and sparkling eyes as she walked to the table where I sat waiting with Rosemarie. She plopped one tulip in front of my place setting and one in front of Rosemarie's then warmly and enthusiastically embraced me. This was my friend, Janice.

The yellow tulip she gave me stands vigilantly in a bud vase beside my laptop. Like a muse, it inspires me to write this story.

A few months ago, while Rosemarie and I were having monthly lunch at Piccolo Forno eatery in Lawrenceville with Karen and Roberta, Rosemarie mentioned her entrepreneurial friend by name. I couldn't believe it was my friend, Janice, too. I asked if she could arrange for a lunch with Janice, Rosemarie, and me. Finally, the day arrived.

I had anticipated this day for two months. We all did. We are all busy women, so it took some doing to coordinate a lunch date we could all make. Finally, the date was made, and the day arrived. I eagerly awaited this visit with great joy.

I had so many salient memories of the times when Janice and I were teaching together in 1972 and later, in the 70s and 80s, when I enjoyed hearing about her three children as they were young and growing up. We laughed a lot as we shared our separate sagas as our lives moved in two different directions—she worked in a family business and I taught at Carlow University. We were quite the lookers in those days; lovely Janice's long auburn hair contrasted with my own medium length blond hair. I would visit her when I observed student teachers in her work neighborhood. The visits stopped when I made a career change and was no longer out in the community with student teachers. As often happens in life, we somehow lost touch over the years.

Now we had the chance to reunite in friendship, orchestrated by our close mutual friend. Rosemarie and I had time together to catch up on things before Janice arrived for lunch. We had not gotten together in more than a month with our monthly foursome at Piccolo Forno. Along with sharing casual conversation, Rosemarie and I had a stimulating conversation about "Shawshank Redemption." We discussed prisons, Pittsburgh writer, John Edgar Wideman, and his brother, who was in prison for life, and prisons and human development in general. Rosemarie commented with sensitive caring, "It seems unfair to give lifetime sentences to adolescents and young adults when their brains are still developing." This conversation grew out of a statement about one Osher lifelong learning course I was attending this semester, Contemporary Pittsburgh Writers. Rosemarie is always interested in what Osher courses I am attending, and they trigger invigorating conversations.

Janice arrived 15 minutes later, and the reunion began. Rosemarie quietly ate and occasionally added a poignant question, insight, or comment. The reunion was Janice's and mine, and it was terrific. We caught up on each other's families. Janice was so proud as she reported on her children. Her son, Thomas Michael, is a filmmaker in New York City who travels the country filming documentaries. Her daughter, Lea, works for Whole Foods in Albuquerque as a marketing director, and her daughter, Sara, is an adjunct professor in Denver teaching education students how to use art with children. I enjoyed their success stories. Tears welled up in me, and I felt proud too. They each grew up well.

Then, I reminisced about taking Lea with me to a restaurant when she was 4- and 5–years-old for a doughnut and milk. Lea would say, "I love you, Ellen," and I loved hearing this. I would follow by taking Lea to my apartment to paint with watercolors. I framed one picture, and Janice told me, "Lea still has it with her, hanging on a wall in her apartment." We continued to talk about her family, and I was amazed that Janice's 94-year-old mother is still living independently. In addition, like my sister, her two sisters lived in Florida. I responded to questions about my sister, proudly telling her that Eileen was a successful nurse educator in Gainesville. She was happy to hear that Eileen's two adopted children were doing well—with husbands and children. Eileen proudly had four grandchildren. Experiencing pride was the feeling of the moment.

We conversed about our current activities. Janice was quite the entrepreneur, owning and selling three businesses in Lawrenceville: a sell-everything shop, a coffee house, and an environmental business. I described my personal life, life story writing, Osher classes, and my volunteer work with Family Hospice .We listened to each other tell our stories intently. The years had not interrupted the love and care we each had for each other.

Two hours later, Rosemarie left to attend to her life. Janice and I remained another hour and talked some more. She is a person who gives to everyone. She is kind and respectful to all; she even greets the poor person walking the street. Sometimes, I get overwhelmed with powerful emotion as I experience, and think about, the sensitively caring friends that I know like Janice. I feel great good fortune for knowing and relating to these wonderful people.

Her children are all grown and on their own, so she is going to do something for herself. She is going on a month-and-a-half retreat to the mountains in Germany to center herself and try writing her story—or anything else she wants to write. Rosemarie and I gave her some advice: write from your heart and take along Julia Cameron's book, *The Artist's Way*, with the valuable recommendation to begin with the three pages of daily, stream of consciousness type, unmonitored writing.

Three hours later, Janice and I leave the restaurant. Shorter hair that had lost its color and a little slower walk marked the aging of these 20 years. But we share a joyful embrace and an "I love you" of reconnecting with a treasured friend. I have missed my friend over the years, and I am delighted to have her back in my life. Again, tears well up in me: can this wonderful event be happening to me—the reunion with a comfortable and loving old friend? I am truly fortunate.

Bourbon Balls

This recipe for Kentucky Bourbon Balls is a version of Janice's treasured recipe and is adapted from one found online at http://allrecipes.com/recipe/Kentucky-bourbon-balls/.

Ingredients:
2 c. chopped nuts
2 16-oz. pkgs confectioner's sugar
3 T Kentucky bourbon
36-oz. semisweet chocolate
1 c. butter, softened

Directions:
Put the nuts in a sealable bottle. Pour the bourbon over the nuts. Seal and let soak overnight.

Mix butter and sugar. Fold in soaked nuts.

Form into ¾" balls. Refrigerate overnight.

Line a tray with waxed paper. Melt the chocolate in a double boiler just barely simmering water, stirring frequently and scraping down the sides with a rubber spatula. Roll the balls in the melted chocolate until coated. Arrange in the prepared tray.

Store in refrigerator until serving.

Yield: 48 balls

A Weighty Topic: Even Healthy Eating Can Be Excessive: Me

I work on showing moderation in my eating.

My visit to Piccolo Forno begins with the tasty and healthy Tuna and Cannellini Bean Salad. This menu item suits me now that I have joined Weight Watchers to lose weight and be healthier. Being in Weight Watchers gives a whole new meaning to the concept of planning and shopping for food. Some say it makes you obsess over food, but I like the program because it encourages planning and exercise. Besides, I can be a little obsessive. Planning involves figuring out healthy menus, shopping carefully, keeping healthy foods in the house, eating plenty of fruits and vegetables, using the internet to find the nutritional values for restaurant menus, and allowing for special occasions. It is not a diet program *per se* but rather an approach to a new, healthier lifestyle.

Food has always been a significant part of my life. I was an anxious child, who was soothed by comfort food. I fought power and control battles over food in childhood—my life was out of control with all of the losses that I experienced, but I could control food intake. From high school on, without realizing it, I continued to be so anxious that I consumed sizable amounts of food and maintained a small size and shapely build. I never knew about the anxiety—it is only upon reflection in psychotherapy in middle life. In my mid 40s when I began taking psychotropic drugs, I began gaining weight. Now, unless I am consciously on an endless diet, I consume too much food as well as gain weight easily from taking the drugs.

Since my middle age, I have been increasingly focused on spending time enjoying food. My friends and I do a lot of visiting over food—dining out and eating in. This is the main entry point for our getting together. Whether it is the eclectic cuisine at Max and Erma's, the hamburgers at River Towne Pour House, the Middle Eastern eats at Ali Baba or the sushi at Taipei Tokyo, we meet and eat as we converse with each other. Our appetites for friendship are as great as our cravings for the foods. We thrive on the camaraderie as much as the diet of delicious treats.

I have always had a penchant for parties, especially with my friends, Dee, Martha, and Sandie. Dee has also had some smaller scale dinner parties. A wonderful soup and salad party at her house included about 15 people. The foods in the next group are not diet foods. Weight Watchers says that you can eat anything so long as you plan ahead for it and observe portion control. At her home, Dee served pumpkin curry, sweet pea and basil, and chicken tortilla soups as the main entrees. Sandie threw a party to welcome Sharon to this country from China. We all enjoyed Martha's recipe for chili as the main course. Dee brought a delicious salad, and Sandie baked corn bread. Martha and Sandie provided for wine. Yes, we all enjoyed dinner parties—attending them or hosting them.

I have included a recipe the Oglebay Four have already tried and loved. This recipe is from the Weight Watchers 3-month tracker* but modified slightly by me. I find it to be a delicious luncheon treat.

Curried Turkey Wrap

Ingredients:
½ c. matchstick carrots
¼ c. reduced-calorie mayonnaise
2 T sugar free apricot preserves
1 t curry powder, yellow variety
3 medium whole wheat tortillas
1-½ c. mixed greens
6 oz. turkey deli meat

Directions:
Mix carrots, mayonnaise, preserves, and curry in a bowl.

Spread ¼ cup of carrot mixture on each tortilla

Place ½ cup of mixed greens on top of spread.

Place 2 oz. of sliced turkey deli meat on top.

Roll each tortilla closed like a standard burrito

Cut each rolled tortilla in half

Yield: 3 whole tortillas

Each whole, filled tortilla counts as a 6 Points Plus value according to Weight Watchers.

*modified from *Weight Watchers 3-Month Tracker*. Weight Watchers International, Inc. ©2011.

WINE AND CHEESE

Enjoying a glass of wine, cheese, or fruit eases the palate before the dinner begins

Special, Supportive Friends

The friends presented in this section have helped clarify life for me.

Doctor. Psychiatrist. Pharmacist. Therapist. Friend. Listener. Advisor: Dr. Hazlett is all of these and more. She is my psychiatrist first but also a friend of sorts. She has to be my doctor first because I need a doctor to guide my medical treatment. After all, I do have a serious medical illness. Yet she treats me in the most caring and compassionate way.

For 20-plus years, Morris has been my friend from Recovery International, a self-help group for nervous persons and those with emotional issues. I flourished under his leadership for many of those years. Shirley is his kind wife whom I have come to know over the years. Morris and Shirley are terrific models for a long-standing, loving marriage.

Lorraine too is my friend of over 20 years from Recovery International. However, like Morris, I have come to see her as my friend, first. So, I also thought of her when I discovered a wonderful recipe for a Middle

Eastern soup, and she liked it too. We talk of many things, and our friendship has broadened over the years.

Dr. Hazlett, Morris and Shirley, and Lorraine all have a special understanding of me, and their relationships have enriched my life.

- **Dr. Hazlett** and I love to make our **Chilled Pea and Basil Soup** for guests.

- **Morris and Shirley** are both wonderful cooks, and they provide a recipe for **Mock Chopped Liver** using a vegetable.

- **Lorraine** selects a special culinary choice which allows her to use fresh rosemary grown in her garden: **Rosemary-Roasted Salmon**.

Another Kind of Teacher: Dr. Hazlett

I come by seeing a psychiatrist legitimately: I'm bipolar, a condition formerly called manic-depressive disorder. Even though diagnosed bipolar at age 43, my psychiatrist says that I probably have been bipolar since childhood. Staying on psychotropic drugs and talking to a psychiatrist weekly keep me mentally healthy. Prior to this regimen, I was hospitalized four times in five years. Both the medicine and the talk therapy together have kept me out of the hospital for 25 years and enabled me to retire as a college professor after 22 years. For this success, I am very grateful.

Whenever I enter Dr. Hazlett's office, I am greeted by a welcoming, "Hi, there." Dr. Hazlett has been my therapist for fifteen years. Because of the many losses in my early childhood, she is sensitive to abandonment as a central theme in the narrative of my life. Tall and slender and nearing her sixty-fifth birthday, Dr. Hazlett's face is kind and has a calm that can turn into a smile when the occasion arises. She is reflective but can be spontaneous.

After my fourth hospitalization, I changed psychiatrists, afraid that, if I didn't, I might end up in a psychiatric hospital for a long period. I was haunted by my mother's 13 year hospitalization. My health insurance referred a psychiatrist—a woman at my request—in a local area of Pittsburgh. Dr. Hazlett was the only woman on the list; fate seemed to be at work here. Although I couldn't really articulate why I was suddenly so fearful that I might end up in the hospital again, Dr. Hazlett agreed to see me.

Now I sit opposite her weekly as we talk—she in a comfortable chair and I on a comfortable, leather couch. I see her face, her torso, and her long legs. Our talks are generally thought-provoking though sometimes they can be more casual because I can be too serious if left to my own designs. Dr. Hazlett often focuses on a theme at the end of each session. In the last session, for example, she pointed out the ways that I protect myself psychologically—taking care of myself. Thinking of the session in those terms was very helpful because I didn't always do that and got into psychological trouble. For example, once I was emotionally raw and yet kept listening to children tell painful personal stories in order to fulfill my consulting contract. Both redirecting the children to tell their stories in more symbolic ways and scheduling the interviews further apart could have kept me psychologically safe. I didn't think of that then; instead, I fell apart. Dr. Hazlett has helped me see my growth in this area, and I have benefitted from these discussions.

In some ways, she is my other Osher Life Long Learning course. Through a discussion of literature, movies, and the theatre, we examine life. She keeps me apprised of what is *au courant* in the world of books, for example. Of course, my discussion gives her insight into issues with me. Plus, it's fun. It taps into my love of literature. I also share with her some of my life story writings as spring boards for conversation. Recipes and cooking are another occasional topic of conversation. Dr. Hazlett loves to cook, and I think she must be very good at it. Interestingly, in retirement, I am getting more involved in cooking myself. Could it be her influence? Recently, for example, she told me of two recipes from Gwyneth Paltrow's new cookbook, and I googled them. One was for cold sweet pea and basil soup. Yummy. The other was for stir-fry chicken with caramelized brown sugar. Delicious. I talk to Dr. Hazlett about cooking, Osher classes, and life story writing, good examples of my outside interests—a terrific tool for my maintaining my mental health. They bring a healthy balance to a straight-forward discussion of my personal issues in our sessions.

Uncharacteristically, several years ago, I called Dr. Hazlett at 4:30 in the morning. She got me through a crisis caused by stresses at the University—she may have even kept me out of the hospital. Highly anxious and over-wrought, I remember speaking with her on the phone a number of times. By talking calmly and adjusting my medication, she alleviated the psychological crisis.

A sensitive and caring person, Dr. Hazlett is also really smart and has a wonderful sense of humor. I like that she's both bright and funny. She is very positive yet realistic, for she recognizes that I am bright and verbal but limited by my background. Her keen insights about my personal life liberate me. Her knowledge about the use of psychotropic drugs supports me. I am very grateful to Dr. Hazlett for being a part of my life, specifically, for aiding me in the healing process by not abandoning me—and for keeping me out of the hospital.

Epilogue: I have begun investigating with her the end of our weekly talk sessions. I think that I am ready. But how do you know when you are ready to leave the home of your loving parents? Dr. Hazlett will not abandon me—she has proven that over and over again. Abandonment means an abrupt and surprise exit from my life. Dr. Hazlett has not done that. I think I need to move forward carrying her wisdom, support, encouragement, and humor inside. Yet I really miss the weekly conversations.

I can continue with her monitoring my medicines—a must! Always the good mother, she will be accessible in case I need to talk. I have proven to be a strong and resilient person. I have the love, support, and friendship of a sister and life-long friends. There is no reason to believe that I can't survive well with them and the internalization of the spirit of Dr. Hazlett.

Yes, over the last two years, I weaned myself from weekly talk therapy to biweekly sessions and frequently to once a month. Dr. Hazlett believed this was a good idea because I brought up the topic for consideration. It was the rapprochement of a separating person—moving away from the good mother to venture out and then returning to refuel. This was a new, forward step in my psychological development—both exciting and scary.

Dr. Hazlett also reminds me that she is always only a phone call away. That assuages my anxiety. Although I've rarely used that privilege in the past it's reassuring to know that I still have it.

Cold Pea and Basil Soup

Ingredients:
1 medium onion, chopped
1 8-oz. bag frozen peas
1-½ t olive oil
2 c. chicken broth
3-5 larger basil leaves

Directions:
Place chopped onions in pan with oil and cook on low heat until tender and translucent.

Simultaneously, place peas in broth. Bring peas and broth to a boil, then reduce heat, and simmer for 10 minutes.

Combine pea mix with onions.

Add basil leaves to mixture. Let cool slightly.

Purée.

Refrigerate and serve cold.

Adapted from (April, 2001). (Gwyneth Paltrow, My father's daughter: Delicious, easy recipes celebrating family and togetherness. New York: Grand Central Life & Style, p. 55.

Stimulating Conversations: Morris and Shirley

Morris and Shirley—a model of a lifelong loving and caring relationship

Morris is my eighty-something friend. A history teacher and swimming coach, he taught in the Pittsburgh City Schools his entire career. I met Morris first at my Recovery International meetings in an Episcopal Church in Squirrel Hill. We both experienced nervous symptoms that created problems with how we felt and functioned. When I told Morris I was in lowered feelings, he would give sage advice: "Wash your car!" I always liked that. We liked each other immediately. We talked about teaching—both of our treasured careers. Through the weekly meetings I attended for over 15 years, we related well, but now our friendship has lasted for over a quarter of a century.

Once I went to Morris's house for dinner. I had the honor of meeting his wonderful and delightful wife, Shirley. I also met a couple, and the husband was my plumber. They entered dressed in black slacks and white, tailored shirts. I thought they were serving food at Morris and Shirley's condo for this small dinner party. Soon I discovered that the couple had just come from ushering at the Pittsburgh Public Theatre and were also guests for dinner.

Two other times, I was honored to be a guest at Morris's celebrations. Once I was invited to a brunch to celebrate his 75th birthday at the Tivoli Restaurant on Rodi Road off of the Parkway East at the Penn Hills exit. Another time, I was pleased to accept an invitation to attend a service and reception at Rodef Shalom Synagogue in Shadyside for Morris's celebration of his 85th birthday. Both occasions allowed me to meet the smart, kind, and gentle people, who are their friends, including his family lawyer and their son, who works as an advocate for low income housing in New York City.

Over the years, I have gotten to know Shirley as well as Morris. She is a bright and compassionate woman. She and Morris have their own educational TV program on cable channel 21 called More Than Learning. Shirley begins each program with the statement, "Learning is not just preparation for life; it is life itself." One episode of their program featured Dr. Twerski, esteemed psychiatrist in the Pittsburgh area, and was the most watched episode. Dr. Twerski talks about people who have influenced him and his projects like the Gateway Center for drug and alcohol rehabilitation.

In addition, another popular program is with Norman Brown, an art educator at Kappa, a Pittsburgh Public School for the arts. He and two colleagues along with Shirley discussed the positive and negative aspects of teaching. One episode is even on YouTube. The Computer Wizard has had 630 viewers. Morris joins Shirley on her shows, but Shirley is the main impetus behind and on the front lines with her show.

I still go to dinner from time to time. I have enjoyed their company at the Olive Garden in Monroeville, Mei Ling's in Homestead, and the Pleasure Bar in Bloomfield. I have wonderful conversations about topics such as what Shirley is reading in her book club, what history books Morris is reading, the meaning of democracy and freedom in America, the educational system including unions and merit pays, the presidential race, Morris's service during World War II in the army air corps, reminisces on growing up Catholic and Jewish, and Jewish customs and traditions. Morris and Shirley are as sharp as tacks. It is a delight to be with them because they are a loving, respectful, and caring couple, who are welcoming to all.

Shirley has a recipe that once was hers, but she now shares with Morris. He makes it.

Mock Chopped Liver

This recipe is made out of green beans, but it tastes just like real chopped liver and is healthier.

Ingredients:
1 T extra virgin olive oil
2 medium onions, chopped
1 can French style green beans
2 hardboiled eggs
¼ cup walnuts
salt and pepper to taste

Directions:
Saute onions in oil until brown.

Drain green beans, pressing out as much water as possible.

Put green beans, eggs, onions and walnuts in food processor and process until smooth.

Add salt and pepper to taste.

*This recipe can be made by vegans by replacing the eggs with fresh mushrooms.

From the Artist's Easel to the Kitchen Pantry: Lorraine

Lorraine hails from Minnesota and handles the Pittsburgh winters well, as you might guess. She is seventy-something and can be found walking all around her neighborhood of Squirrel Hill every season of the year, including winter. Although slight of build, she is a hearty individual.

I met Lorraine in Recovery International nearly 20 years ago. We were both nervous persons, and this was a self-help group for us. The members of the group all love Lorraine's comments that show much insight. She is kind, patient, and helpful as she points out Recovery slogans such as "Imagination on fire" or "The need to use objectivity."

We have continued our weekly meetings over the years though I come much less frequently now. When I began attending the meetings and for the next 14 years, I lived in Morningside and Shadyside, so it was convenient to meet in Squirrel Hill. I saw Lorraine weekly. Now, I live in Monroeville, quite a ways from Squirrel Hill. I drive into the city much less frequently for the meetings. However, Lorraine and I have maintained our friendship.

Lorraine is a visual artist. In fact, I have a picture that she created for me as a present. It hangs in my living room. It has warm shades of browns and oranges, bold aquamarine and occasional traces of pale violet and is called "Signs of Spring." Lorraine dresses like an artist in vests, scarves and sweaters of interesting colors that accent her cosmopolitan outfits. She always dresses smartly.

Lorraine and I sometimes meet for coffee and conversation in Café 61C in Squirrel Hill. She sips her cappuccino, and I drink my latte as we converse about our Osher classes, her family, her grandchildren, the art projects she is working on, and my current writing activities. Our discussions conclude an hour or so later after she has used a spoon to get the foamed cream from her cup of the remaining cappuccino.

Lorraine and I had season tickets for the opera for several years. We dressed up—as our generation still does for the opera—and ate first at Amoré, an upscale restaurant in Oakland, and then proceeded to the opera for a feast in beautiful music—*belle conte*. We had seats high in the Benedum Hall, but it didn't matter. The acoustics are so excellent that the musical experience is wonderful from any seat.

We sometimes exchange recipes. I came across an interesting recipe for a Moroccan harira soup—a soup with lamb, lentils, tomatoes, chickpeas, noodles, and Middle Eastern seasonings like coriander, turmeric, and curry. I sent the recipe to Lorraine thinking that she might enjoy it. She said that she did and could modify the seasonings somewhat to suit her tastes—I don't know enough about cooking to do that yet. She has included a recipe here, one of her favorites.

Rosemary-Roasted Salmon

Ingredients:
2 bunches fresh rosemary
1 large red onion (or regular onion), sliced
1 or 2 lb. salmon filets with skin, cut in 4 individual
  serving pieces
olive oil
salt
pepper
1 or 2 lemons, sliced

Directions:
Preheat oven to 400 degrees.

Arrange ½ of rosemary in single layer in 4 areas of
baking pan.

Arrange onion on top of rosemary

Place salmon, skin side down, on onion. Sprinkle salt
and pepper. Cover salmon with remaining rosemary.

Arrange lemon slices over rosemary. Drizzle olive oil
over. Sprinkle lemon slices with salt.

(Can be prepared 8 hours ahead of time and covered in
refrigerator.)

Roast salmon, uncovered, until just cooked, about 20
minutes.

Transfer salmon to plates, serve with the roasted onions
and lemon slices.

Yield: 4 servings

SOUP

This healthy comfort food starts the meal, wakens the taste buds, and encourages a liberal spirit, just as my early adulthood did.

College Friends

Wordsworth and Coleridge. T. S. Elliot. Supreme court decisions. Existential philosophers. Existential psychologists. World Cultures. Trigonometry. Freud. Composition writing. Biology. The liberal arts education I received enriched my life forever. Being an undergraduate at Duquesne University provided a wonderful balance between intellectual stimulation and social activity. The backdrop of Duquesne enveloped me in a caring environment on campus from the dorms to the cafeterias to the grottos where people sat and talked. Also I found one social niche there, the local, Catholic social sorority, Alpha Phi Omicron, to give expression to my fellowship needs.

In love with life and my new found freedom with some guidelines, I discovered a happiness and joy I had never known before in a solitary state. So much was new and exciting and singular.

My senior sorority picture

I had a terrific home at Duquesne University and lived on campus for three and one half years. It was fun meeting a somewhat diverse group of students there—more diverse than I had ever known.

Food was unimportant to me at that time. I continued to be a picky eater but ate what I wanted in the cafeteria. No one pressured me to eat. I did not eat healthily, but I ate enough to survive just fine. However, on Sunday early evenings, after Mass at Epiphany Church in the Hill, a group of my friends and I went to dinner at Bubbles and Sherman Restaurant on Fifth Avenue near Duquesne University. Every week, surly wait staff would serve my favorite—a bowl of matzo ball soup and a kosher roast beef sandwich on a heel of rye bread with a kosher dill pickle. Eating at this wonderful Jewish deli broadened my palate to include something other than hamburgers and fries.

Steve and Charlie were good friends to me in college. I met Sue at Duquesne but really became friends with her after graduation when we roomed together. She was my dinner and game partner. A proud

Briton, she shared traditional English cooking with me. Rosemary and Richard are two friendships that I have continued to enjoy since my undergraduate college days. Rosemary and I meet on a regular basis to have lunch and talk. Richard and I, too, have lengthy conversations over food and wine—and about the arts. We also thrive on our discussions of our courses that we take at the University of Pittsburgh. Loving the classroom and the role of the student, we share these cherished moments.

- **Rosemary** includes a delicious recipe for **Cranberry Bread** which she brought with her from her life as a young mother living in Rhode Island.

- **Richard** has chosen to have me include my recipe for **Stuffed Cabbage** rather than a recipe of his own. It is a celebratory food for him that also reminds him of his mother who once made this. The aromas upon entering my home conjure up treasured memories.

- **Sue** loved her English heritage and enjoyed sharing it with others. She would have been pleased that her **Shepherd's Pie** recipe is part of this book.

- **Steve & Charlie** were specifically part of my transition from living with my relatives to living on my own after college—and making a healthy adjustment to it. When they visited over Christmas break, Eileen and I offered them **Ham and Salami Sandwiches** on small **Rye Bread and Cheese Pastries**.

Life Can Be Full of Surprises: Rosemary

Rosemary and I have a long history together including college, sorority, roommates, and friends.

Rosemary called to say, "Hello." We had a long history as friends beginning in college. We met at Duquesne University when I helped her move into the dorms her first year, a year after me. Now, we did not see each other as often as we once had. Our lives had just become busy in different directions. Back in 1988, she had a husband and children. I had a job and had recently completed a PhD. But we kept in touch and always could be counted on. It was fortuitous that she called.

As we talked, I began unfolding the saga of my recent job. I was a wait staff at a local family restaurant in Penn Hills—that is until the week before. One evening, the owner was drunk and yelled, "Come here, Ellen, and sit down. I want to talk to you about the waitresses."

I said, "I'll talk to you tomorrow when you are sober. I'm done, so I'm leaving now."

He screamed in fury, "If you leave, don't come back!"

I told Rosemary that I had driven home crying and I didn't know why. I had done nothing wrong. He was verbally abusive to me.

But I was scared. I needed a job to take care of myself. I owed rent, had food and utilities to pay for. What could I do? I was crying. I had gone out every day to get another wait staff job, but I still had not succeeded. I was frightened that I would not be able to take care of myself. My bouts at WPIC had undermined my self-confidence. Jobs as wait staff were not easy to come by, at least not ones that earned enough to enable a person to live on her own.

Then Rosemary told me about an opportunity where she worked at Wesley Highlands School for students with special emotional needs. They needed day-to-day substitutes in classrooms for all ages. They paid $45.00 a day. I had a car, old though it was, and could do that. I called that day and began substituting soon after. I was called to come in nearly every day since I could comfortably work in any classroom and with all ages. Now, I had some income to begin paying my bills, but I needed more. I would work on that. In the meantime, Rosemary and I began renewing our friendship on a daily basis. This was January 1988.

Within a month, a teacher in the high school left, and I was put in her classroom—with Rosemary as the classroom assistant. We were even working as a team together now. What fun. Also, I soon found a job as a wait staff in the evening from 4:30 PM to midnight at Brandie's in the Strip District, downtown. It was a wonderful restaurant with excellent food, a fine menu, a kind Harvard graduate owner, and a wait staff of college graduates, who had no idea what to do with the rest of their lives. I was a college graduate and former teacher, who was a recent graduate of WPIC and was trying to get my life back together.

Life went on very well. I was fine financially— able to pay my bills. I had a full time job that enabled me to make my transition back to a professional career after being hospitalized. Rosemary and I were enjoying our renewed friendship. On June 16, we celebrated Rosemary's birthday in each of our five classes. Unknown to Rosemary, I brought in five large bottles of pop, five delicious birthday cakes from Giant Eagle's bakery, and some bags of ice. I was ready for the surprise. The kitchen staff let me store the cakes, pop, and ice.

Beginning first period in the morning, I brought out the first cake and we sang "Happy Birthday" to Rosemary. Then Rosemary cut the cake. She did not know I had five cakes and obviously thought I only had one. The cake had about 12-15 pieces in it. However, Rosemary cut it in sliver-thin slices for the teens, so there would be some left over for the other classes. I smiled inside at this.

When the kids asked, "Can I have another piece of cake?" I said, "Sure"—much to Rosemary's dismay—and I proceeded to cut each of them a regular size piece of cake. They were now satisfied.

When the second class came in, I produced a new, second birthday cake with "Happy Birthday, Rosemary" written on it, and we sang the birthday song. Now Rosemary could cut each of the teens a typical size of cake with a free conscience. We followed this celebration procedure all day long for five class periods—and with five cakes. Rosemary and I were wired from the sugar and the excitement as the day went on, but nevertheless we enjoyed the parties. Life is just full of surprises.

Before the school year was over, Wesley Highlands School offered me a position as a full time high school English teacher. I couldn't believe I was back in academia after my experiences at WPIC three times. I don't know that I would have ever had the confidence to apply for a teaching position, but because I came in as a day-to-day substitute, I could try on the job, and I built up my confidence. Rosemary had been instrumental in helping me feel more confident by telling me about the position, having faith that I could do it, and just treating me like a regular person.

More amazing, before I signed the contract, I applied for and got a position at Carlow University. I now had the confidence to seek out a professional job. I considered myself very fortunate as I contacted

Wesley Highland and informed them of my situation and desires. They were very kind and understanding and could hire another teacher easily at this time. I went to Carlow, where I planned all summer in my office for my classes and administrative responsibilities. But I left at 4:00 PM for my 4:30 PM wait staff job at Brandie's, an upscale restaurant in the Strip District. I would do this until I received my first pay check from Carlow.

Rosemary enabled me to have these experiences and these choices. She has been a good and loyal friend over almost five decades. She is a fiercely independent woman. I see her from time to time again, but we know that we can count on each other. I consider myself very fortunate to know Rosemary; she has impacted my life strongly. Who would have thought that, when we began that conversation on the phone 25 years ago, Rosemary would have been so important in getting me back into academia? Like Rosemary's multiple birthday cakes, life can be full of surprises for people who are open to them. On the other hand, if you know what a caring and supportive friend Rosemary is, it is no surprise that Rosemary and I have been friends for many years and that we will continue on into the future.

Cranberry Bread

Rosemary shares, "I acquired this recipe from a good friend while living in Rhode Island over 30 years ago. I have made this cranberry bread recipe every Christmas for the last 30 years and given it away as a Christmas gift. Every time I make the recipe, it reminds me of the great times I had living in Rhode Island. Hope you enjoy it as much as I and my friends have for a long time."

Ingredients:
2 c. flour
1 c. sugar
½ t salt
½ c milk
2 eggs
1 stick butter, melted
1 c. cranberries, rinsed
Cooking spray for greasing the pan

Directions:
Mix dry ingredients thoroughly.

Add milk, then eggs one at a time.

Add melted butter.

Add cranberries.

Grease the pan or spray with cooking spray.

Bake at 350 degrees for approximately 30 to 45 minutes.

Winning Isn't All: Sue

Sue and Richard, college classmates, at a party

Sue could make you laugh easily. She would pick up in her hands a Yahtzee that I just threw, exactly as they had landed, for example, shake her hands with the dice unmoved, place the dice on the table, and exclaim, "Yahtzee!" I'd laugh every time she did it—never tiring of her silly antics. Although Sue and I attended the symphony together for 17 years, I most remember her for our years of game nights at her house in Oakmont.

For many years, when her husband, Dick, went out of town weekly, I spent the evening with her. We would have dinner first. Sue cooked an English meal of meat, potatoes, and a vegetable. She introduced me to Yorkshire and plum puddings. She was very English, proud of it, and loyal to the royal family. She followed the Queen's activities and watched Princess Diana's wedding as a patriot. Although Sue had immigrated to the U.S. with her family as a youngster, she was still very proud to be English. She even returned to live in England for a time while contemplating retaining her English citizenship. Ultimately she chose to come back to the States and obtain U.S. citizenship.

Now that Sue had settled back in the U.S. and married Dick, she began having me over for dinners when Dick traveled to West Virginia for work. After dinner, we would get out the games. Yahtzee, Monopoly, and Canasta were our favorites. I was competitive in Yahtzee but a dismal failure in Monopoly. Sue would even stop trying to win and give me a chance to catch up in Monopoly, but I rarely did. I usually owned and had motels on the ghetto properties of Baltic Avenue and Mediterranean Avenue.

We were equally competitive in Canasta, and we both enjoyed a good card game for a change. We always had to use Hoyle's book of card game directions to remind us of how to play the game. We also sometimes played Gin. Eventually, Sue introduced me to Cribbage. We would spend hours in the evening playing games and laughing. Throughout the evenings, music played in the background. We listened to rock or classical—Sue was quite as eclectic in her music selection as she was in her reading.

Sue later died of complications from heart surgery. I miss playing games with her. I selected Shepherd's Pie as her recipe. It represents the English heritage which she loved, and I fondly remember her making it for dinner with me.

Shepherd's Pie

Ingredients:
4 white potatoes, peeled, diced, boiled and mashed
2 t parsley flakes
1 lb. ground beef, cooked and chunked
¼ c chopped onion
2 c canned corn

Directions:
Heat oven to 350 degrees.

In a 3-quart, greased casserole pan, layer the total full quantity of meat, followed by corn and then mashed potatoes.

Bake for 30 minutes or until potatoes are slightly golden.

Culture and Cuisine: Richard

*Me and Richard enjoying a meal at a local
Pittsburgh eatery*

Richard was lying on the couch in a semi-sleep state. I got my three-foot stuffed, floppy dog, went over to him, and had the dog sing him a wake up tune—to the tune of "Wake Up Little Suzie" by the Everly Brothers.

> "Wake up little Richard, wake up.
> Wake up little Richard, wake up.
> The talk with Janet was hot.
> You'd think we had a plot.
> You fell asleep.
> Your goose is cooked.
> Your reputation is shot.
> Wake up little Richard.
> Wake up little Richard.
> You gotta go home."

I had just finished college. I was in a social sorority, and this is the kind of thing I could do. This was Richard's introduction to me. He was shy, and I didn't know that.

Richard had just returned from Mexico where he had spent a year on a Fulbright in 1966. He was visiting my roommate, Janet. They had talked until early morning, and Richard had fallen asleep on the couch. Janet was making breakfast, and I was being silly. Richard, however, did not show any sign of being impatient with me—amazing now that I think of it.

A year later, after Janet had married Dan, Richard and I started doing things together. Richard was handsome in an Italian way, and he was bright and articulate. Passionate about the arts, he was my cultural guide. He introduced me to opera, and we had season subscriptions to the theatres. We went to arts films and to popular movies.

Part of our ritual was to eat out after each event, and our choices matched our budgets. When we began our cultural adventure with foreign films, first, we ate at Wendy's, imbibing volumes of Frosties, and at Eat 'N Park, consuming tanks of chili. We went to the movies, but we were poor. Nevertheless, we enjoyed the conversations about each film and talking about teaching too—we were both dedicated teachers.

Once, several years later, we splurged and ate at the Cheese Cellar in Station Square having wine, cheese, grapes, and French bread.

During a very comfortable conversation for me, Richard stated "I just wanted you to know that I'm gay." I now understood why he was friendly but distant to a degree with me.

I commented, "I appreciate your honesty. It helps me to understand you better." There was a great stigma involved with that then—still is to some degree. But I was disappointed too since I had envisioned him as a person to date.

Richard reflected "I wish everyone was as understanding as you are."

Our conversation continued at length about what it meant to be a gay man. We became closer that day because of this sincere dialogue. Food, conversation, and wine seem to lend themselves to that.

As the years progressed, we began to go to the Pittsburgh Public Theatre and to the City Theatre. Now we chose such restaurants as Bravo, Tambellini on Seventh Street in downtown, and Paparazzi on the South Side. Richard introduced me to Osso Buco, veal shank on a bone at Tambellini, and to Pasta Diablo, pasta with a hot sauce, at Paparazzi. Lidia's in the Strip District also proved to be a delight as we enjoyed all-you-could-eat of three pastas accompanied by delectable breads with wonderful seasoned oil dips—and, of course, good wines. The food improved as the years passed and our incomes increased. And Richard and I continued to be passionate about the arts and the food.

Now our favorites are Ali Baba in Oakland on Craig Street, with Middle Eastern cuisine, and Piccolo Forno, a Tuscan eatery in Lawrenceville. Although our incomes have diminished with retirement, our appetites for delicious food have not. We have found moderately-priced restaurants to suit us. The conversations between Richard and me have continued for over 45 years, and his passion still pours forth.

Richard loves my stuffed cabbage, so I make it for him for his birthday in December. He really shows his appreciation in a very Italian, expressive way full of sighs and hand gestures, thus, he's a delight to cook for. Richard brings the bottle of wine. Good friends, good food, good conversation, and good wine—is there anything better?

My Stuffed Cabbage

Ingredients:

2 heads of cabbage, cut slightly around the stalk
3 lbs. ground beef
1¼ c. rice (not Minute)
1 large onion, chopped
salt
pepper
garlic powder
3 eggs
1 12-oz. small can tomato sauce
1 46-oz. bottle tomato juice and extra for thinning
   sauce
1 c. V-8

Directions:

In a large pot, boil 2 cabbages only enough to loosen leaves.

Do not dump water. Remove cabbages from pot. Being careful not to tear them, peel off 20-25 of the largest leaves.

Slice remaining cabbage to a sauerkraut (or slightly wider) thickness.

Pour out all but 1½ inches of cabbage water from the pot. Mix in tomato sauce.

Fill 1/3 of each cabbage leaf with raw meat filling (meat, rice, seasoning). Roll shut, stuffing the ends of the leaf inside the roll.

Place rolls back in the large pot. Add tomato juice, V-8, and sliced cabbage. Simmer for 3-4 hours. Add additional tomato juice as needed.

Serve with parsley potatoes or mashed potatoes and French bread.

Transition from Family to Friends: Me

I cannot forget the difficulty of Christmases past. Families of friends were very protective of having Christmas day with only their families when I was in my late teens and twenties. I struggled with this exclusion for a number of years. Then I found my own way. It has been evolving ever since then.

Christmas Day and Nowhere to Go: Me

To reiterate, when I was a child and adolescent, I had a large family of five married aunts, two married uncles, and five cousins, who got together for the holiday. No matter which part of the family my sister and I lived with, we were a part of the holiday mix. Different relatives hosted the various celebrations and did all of the cooking. They were festive times with plenty of delicious food—tender and juicy turkey, candied yams, creamy mashed potatoes, sweet cranberry sauce, tasty vegetables, and homemade cookies of all sorts—and laughter and joy led by Aunt Molly and Uncle Leonard. Even when I lived with mean Aunt Julia in high school, holidays were happy because the whole family was together. I'm sure that Aunt Julia had a story that accounted for her meanness. But Eileen and I were the children, and she was the adult. The onus to cope was on her, not us. Nevertheless, the family was fun to be with over the holidays. Then I went off to college.

Christmas was the toughest time of my life for years. Since Aunt Julia was the last one I lived with, she expected me to come home to her house for each holiday. I sure did not consider it to be my *home*. As far as I saw it, I had no *home*. Well, after the freedom and joyfulness of being in college, her house had a great pall over it. I came to Aunt Julia's house the first year of college for all vacations because Eileen was in her senior year in high school and still living there. I didn't want to abandon her.

Transitions can be difficult. The transition from living with relatives to living on my own was generally wonderful at Duquesne, but there were difficult times. I had to face the ghosts from my past. When Eileen went away to nursing school the next year, we did not want go to Aunt Julia's for the holidays. But Aunt Julia made it very clear to the relatives that we must go to her house for the holidays or nowhere. She was very controlling, and they were scared of her—I'm not sure why. So no one ever invited us to their houses for the holidays. These were painfully difficult times for me. While all of the holidays were a challenge for me, Christmas was especially hard.

Every year, as Thanksgiving passed and the celebration of Christmas began, I felt so alone. When there was the annual Christmas concert at Duquesne University, I got teary-eyed throughout but particularly as they sang, "There's No Place Like Home for the Holidays," "I'm Dreaming of a White Christmas," and "I'll Be Home for Christmas." I had no home. I belonged nowhere. During these years in my late teens and twenties, I was depressed from Thanksgiving on.

Eileen and I still had each other and tried to cope with the Christmas blues together. Eileen came to Pittsburgh and, each year, friends of mine from college lent me an apartment—a student that was going home for the Christmas vacation. Eileen and I would clean this student apartment and then we'd go to shop for a lot of food. We had a clean house and food. We were ready for the Christmas holiday as best as we knew.

But Eileen and I were still sad. We didn't know how to enjoy Christmas together. But there was a good part to this story that included a friend of mine, Charlotte. The dorms were closed for the Christmas vacation, and Charlotte was remaining in Pittsburgh for three extra days to work. When I saw her, she was leaving Duquesne for a room that she was going to rent during vacation while she worked. I invited her to stay with Eileen and me and gave her my phone number in case she changed her mind.

A day later, Charlotte called to say that she would like to stay with us. She told us that when she went to rent her room, she was refused and spent the night in the YWCA. You see, Charlotte was black. We welcomed her and enjoyed her company when she was free from working. She gave us a copy of *The Family of Man,* a beautiful book of inspirational thoughts and poems, as a thank you present. With Charlotte, we talked, laughed, told stories and generally enjoyed each other before she went home for Christmas.

Eileen and I went to midnight mass at Duquesne University on Christmas Eve. Then we cooked a turkey and prepared all of the trimmings on Christmas day. But we spent the day lying around being sad because we had no family to share Christmas with. I had friends in Pittsburgh that we could have invited over for a visit during these two weeks. I think Eileen and I would have liked that. However, I was too ashamed of not having a family to go to for Christmas. I did not want to let others know that Eileen and I were alone. We were depressed.

We would have to go off on our own to develop friendships and discover how to enjoy Christmas as adults without a family—or with a newly formed family. Then we could come back together and share the Christmas holiday. This would come to pass.

Eileen and I spent many long hours on many visits with each other in our 20s putting together 1,000-piece jigsaw puzzles—maybe a metaphor for our solving our life's personal puzzles.

Eileen's Christmas Turkey

Eileen cooked the Christmas turkey that we had, and I was her assistant. We had a full turkey dinner, but I will include only the recipe for the turkey with her special seasoning and stuffing.

Ingredients:
8-12 lb. turkey, thawed, cleaned, and rinsed with cold water
1 large onion, cut in quarters
6-8 garlic cloves
salt
pepper
garlic salt
stuffing (see recipe below)
1/8 c. olive oil

Directions:
Season inside with quartered onion, garlic cloves, and salt and pepper.

Stuff with stuffing.

Rub olive oil on breast of turkey.

Sprinkle salt, pepper, and garlic salt liberally on breast of turkey, rubbing it both on and under the skin.

Cover with foil and bake according to the schedule on the turkey wrapper.

Uncover last 45 minutes to brown.

Let sit 20 minutes before carving.

Eileen's Turkey Stuffing

Ingredients:
2 12-oz. pkg. herb and sage stuffing mix (bread cubes)
4 eggs, beaten
2 c. chicken broth
1 medium chopped onion
salt and pepper
3 garlic cloves, minced

Directions:
Mix ingredients together, adding chicken broth a little at a time until the consistency is mushy but not watery.

Stuffing may be used inside turkey or around the turkey and baked according to the directions for the turkey.

To bake stuffing outside of a bird, place stuffing in a separate 9" x 13" pan. Bake 45 minutes in a 325-degree oven and until browned

The Gift: Steve and Charlie

The dorms were closing for Christmas break, as usual, when I was a junior at Duquesne University in 1965. What to do? My sister, Eileen, and I didn't have any family to stay with: we had been raised by a Grandpa who died and several aunts and uncles. The family situation was uninviting and ultimately unhealthy, and Eileen and I wanted a change.

A solution appeared. Two of my friends, John and Dave, from college offered Eileen and me their apartment in Shadyside. They were two Alpha Epsilon social fraternity brothers, brothers of the social sorority that I belonged to. They would be going home for the holidays and the apartment would be free. I was very fortunate to have such generous and sensitive friends.

Eileen rode a Greyhound bus from nursing school in Cleveland, Ohio, to Pittsburgh, and I met her at the station. We schlepped her luggage to the apartment and settled her in. Eileen and I, in the way we were brought up, scrubbed this apartment to spotlessness—after all it was usually being inhabited by two college men.

Then we proceeded to the large and varied Diamond Market in Market Square, downtown Pittsburgh, to buy food for our two-week stay. We delighted in buying all kinds of food like turkey and trimmings for Christmas Day and fresh cold meats and Jewish rye bread for sandwiches. We spent $100.00—a lot of money in those days. We returned to the apartment in a cab—there were simply too many bags of food to carry on a bus—and enjoyed stocking the refrigerator and shelves.

Now we were ready to settle in for the holidays. What to do? Just then, we heard a knock on the door. When I opened it, I stared facing a tall, lovely spruce tree. Holding it up was my friend from college, Steve. Next to him was Charlie, his roommate and another friend of mine from college. Charlie was holding a paper bag. Steve carried the six foot tree in and set it up in the living room on a stand they brought. Charlie removed the string of lights from the bag, and they strung them on the tree. Steve commented, "It's the most beautiful Christmas tree I ever saw." And, indeed, it was.

Steve and Charlie stayed to visit for a while. We enjoyed conversation over the little sandwiches Eileen and I had carefully made from what we had just purchased; the party Jewish rye, slices of salami and ham and mustard were a hit. The camaraderie was good. Steve and Charlie shared an apartment off campus at Duquesne University and were two years older than me. Both were history and secondary education majors—having teaching to fall back on if they needed to while working to get through law school. I spent many an evening during my sophomore year at their apartment listening to Frank Sinatra, drinking beer, and talking about life. They were like the brothers I never had. Yes, I was lucky to have such good friends in my life. What a gift.

Party Rye Sandwiches

As was our habit, Eileen and I always offered food to guests who might drop by to our homes. We did this with everyone, always. We offered Charlie and Steve sandwiches and coffee.

We all enjoyed the repast and the conversation as the gathering continued. In the greater scheme of things, these kinds of events helped to provide the transition from a stressful childhood and adolescence to a healthier adulthood.

Ingredients:
sliced party rye bread
sliced salami and ham
mustard
kosher pickles
cheese cake pastries
cups of coffee

Directions:
Make sandwiches using rye, lunchmeat, and mustard. Cut them to the desired sizes. Arrange them on plates with pickles and pastries.

Serve with coffee.

Christmas Day and Nowhere to Go (part 2): Me

My first oil painting of my left foot that I did on a Christmas when I was alone in my 20s. I found a way to entertain myself, get involved and get rid of the Christmas blues.

In my early 20s, Christmas was the one day a year where I was not welcomed anywhere that I knew of. My friends were all with their families, and Christmas was a family occasion. I could come over to their houses the day before or the day after, but Christmas day was exclusively for the family. This was my experience. It depressed me.

I would be depressed from Thanksgiving until after Christmas day. It made me feel keenly aware that I belonged nowhere for the holiday. It never dawned on me to work on getting married and to start my own family. Now I know, subconsciously, I was afraid of mental illness following the birth of a child—post-partum depression, nameless and unknown to me at the time. Nevertheless, I just always felt left out of the Christmas celebration that my friends were enjoying.

Then, in my middle and late 20s, after several years of feeling sorry for myself, I realized that I had to figure out a better way to cope with being alone on Christmas day. I decided to treat myself to a new experience each year. The first year, I bought oil paints, brushes, canvases, and an easel, and on Christmas day, I introduced myself to the pleasures of oil painting. I loved it, totally immersed myself and enjoyed the day. Amazing! I had found a solution to my dilemma. Initially, I didn't know what to paint. Then I looked down, saw the toes on my left foot and painted a stylized version of them in shades of green. It is still hanging in my house. Every year, I provided myself with a new, solitary adventure.

As life would have it, after a few years, I began getting invitations for Christmas day dinners. My friend, Sue, whose family lived in Canada, suggested that we share a dinner together. She worked and didn't have time to drive up to her family's home. I offered to cook, and we decided we wanted steak. That's what we had. It was delicious, and the conversation was lively.

We also played Yahtzee and Monopoly. Sue and I enjoyed playing games. It was so pleasurable to have some company on Christmas—just simple fun.

As I reached my late 20s, Sue was taken away for Christmas by demands as a ministry student, but then Dianne entered the picture. Dianne's mother was an orphan and was sensitive to being without a family especially for the holidays. She made sure that Dianne invited me over for every holiday. We had the traditional turkey and trimmings. I brought the pumpkin pies. All was delicious, and, again, it was so good to have the company. We ate and watched the holiday programs on TV. Simple pleasures.

In my 30s, and after a few years with Dianne and her parents, I had two holiday invitations. Now Dianne and her parents invited me to Christmas and so did my oldest friend, Janet. Janet had Christmas dinner at 2:00 PM and Dianne had it at 6:00 PM—and they lived near each other. I treated myself and went to both. What is it they say about feast or famine?

Then, in my mid-40s, Eileen moved to West Lafayette, Indiana, for five years while her roommate, Silvia, got her PhD. Now I had my sister to spend my holidays with. It was fun to have her and her children so near. I could and did drive there for every holiday. I delighted in spending Christmas's baking Russian tea balls, cooking a traditional turkey dinner, sharing a Cuban Christmas eve meal with Silvia and her parents, and watching Eileen's young daughters open mounds of Christmas presents. Eileen was effusive in giving toys and clothes to the children. We also would play Bingo with prizes of tablets, pens, and pencils—my favorites. It brought out the school teacher in me. We would also visit her friends and share the holiday cheer.

Both Eileen and I had learned how to enjoy Christmas by spending time with our friends. We had come a long way from the sad young women of our teens and our 20s. Now we could be together and enjoy the Christmas season by including each other, our friends and our family. We each created our family of friends.

Fruit and Cheese Board

On these alone days, I grazed on simple foods to keep my energy up during my creative activities.

Ingredients:
bunch of green grapes
bunch of red grapes
wedge of muenster cheese
round of smoked gouda cheese
assorted crackers
an apple
bottle cabernet sauvignon

Directions:
Slice apple. Arrange ingredients attractively on a cheese board.

SALAD

The greens of new experiences nourished me and provided growth.

Recipes from My London Friends

Miss Muriel Finch's lodge was three blocks from Tony's restaurant and yet, to my knowledge, Tony and Miss Finch never met. But they knew of each other. Miss Finch's lodgers went to Tony's restaurant for occasional meals—Italian, of course. Over tasty food, they discussed the day's touring, the interesting encounters on the Tube ride, the invigorating concerts in the park and the friendliness of the English people when it was off season for tourists. These travelers who stayed at the lodge often finished their meal with a cup of British tea—automatically served white unless you asked for tea without milk. They also talked about Miss Muriel Finch and her extraordinarily clean, comfortable, and quaint lodge. Yes, Miss Muriel Finch and Tony may never have met, but they were intertwined by virtue of their respective vocations.

- **Miss Muriel Finch's English Breakfast** started us each day in the lodge as we congregated to eat and chat about the day's adventures.

- **Tony's Spaghetti and Meatballs** graced many tables at the eatery as tourists and locals talked over the day's events.

Being Entrepreneurial: Miss Finch and Tony

Chaucer, Shakespeare, Dickens, the Globe Theatre, the London Bridge were all a part of my literary background. I was a high school English teacher who was in love with teaching British literature, and I found myself thinking of London where *Macbeth*, a musical version of *The Canterbury Tales*, and *Oliver!* were all playing. A trip there sounded appealing to me in 1971.

Fielding's's Guide to Travel in Europe proved to be a very good source. I used it to select a place to stay while visiting London. It was less popular than *Europe on Five Dollars a Day* and probably easier to book a hotel or lodge from. I was 25-years-old and planning a three month trip. I was looking for comfort, economy, safety, and proximity to the city. Although three settings sounded appealing, Wysall Lodge stood out. Located in West Hampstead, a twenty minute Tube ride to Piccadilly Circus, it was close to the action of London. Described as quaint, it had 12 rooms, several singles and several doubles, a public bath, a dining area with breakfast included, and a bright and airy environment. The proprietor, Miss Muriel Finch, sold me on the lodge. She sounded very maternal as she wrote me, "You will have a comfortable room and a place where you would be safe and well taken care of." This appealed to me as a lone traveler. The price was also reasonable, so I confirmed Wysall Lodge.

Miss Muriel Finch greeted me at the door—tall and thin, with blond, curly hair, and with a dress and apron. She smiled welcomingly, and I felt at home immediately. Although she was on pension and in her mid-70s, she spryly led me up the stairs to my second floor room. It was all white with sunlight coming in the window and a single bed and a dresser. A coin operated heater was in the wall for chilly nights and mornings. Yes, it was comfortable and would be my home for the next three months.

In the mornings, breakfast was served to the ten or so residents between 7:00 AM and 9:00 AM. by Miss Finch. The dining room had some two-seat tables, some four-tops, and one longer table—welcoming all configurations of guests. Heaters in the wall spaced throughout the room took the chill out. Miss Finch cooked and served eggs and sausage or bacon and toast with coffee. It tasted quite delicious. Some mornings, she added oatmeal as an option. French, Spanish, South Africans, Americans, and Canadians were residents. We had some wonderful conversations over a leisurely breakfast. I delighted in the cosmopolitan group. Sharing our sightseeing adventures with each other was fun. For example, we talked of Henry VIII's growing armor as he aged and the modern rendition of *Macbeth* with yellow slickers and machine guns at the new Globe Theatre. And we'd talk about our lives in each of our countries. We grew quite fond of each other even in the short time together.

After breakfast, I would leave West Hampstead for the day. First though, I would go to the friendly local store and get an apple, some digestive cookies, a hunk of cheese, and a beverage. No matter where you go in London, there is a park within walking distance, so I would bring my lunch. I would pick the play that I would see and go to the Tube station where the theatre was located. During the day, I would see the sights in that area of London. I loved the richness of history and especially literature everywhere in London. I walked down streets that Shakespeare walked, sat under a tree Thomas More sat under, explored Thomas Carlyle's home, and visited many book shops on Fleet Street. And I would see my daily live theatre matinee. I felt alive and at home in such a literary city—after all literature was my life and livelihood.

A few blocks down the street from the cozy Wysall Lodge stood a small, quaint Italian Restaurant, Tony's—of course. Tony, the svelte, middle-aged proprietor, was present every day and active about the business of running the eatery. He would always stop to greet each customer. Nearly every night, my Tube ride home ended at Tony's. I came in for a hot, substantial Italian dinner at a very reasonable price. Traveling alone, I often ate dinner by myself, so Tony sometimes sat with me for a while. The conversation was always friendly and comfortable. Tony made me feel welcome.

On one particular night, I was waiting for my dinner and talking with Tony as he hand printed clip-ons of specials for the menu. He added *patat*. I teased that in England it was potato. He pointed out that in Italy it was *patat*. I mentioned that we were in England. We enjoyed a good laugh. I then asked if I could write the clip-ons for him, and he agreed. Using my best script writing learned in high school calligraphy class, I scripted each clip-on neatly and attractively—and in English. Tony was noticeably impressed. Then my dinner of spaghetti and meatballs with a small amount of sauce was served—to this day, I prefer small portions of sauce on my spaghetti. A delicious meal and good conversation followed.

At the end of my dinner, Tony made me an offer: "If you will create seven menus for me, I will give you two weeks of free dinners at the restaurant." My budget was tight, so it was a great offer. Also, I liked doing calligraphy and painting. I befriended Bob, a London business man, who helped me get the supplies. He provided large sheets of white paper. I purchased a pen and ink very cheaply as well as a water color set like you use in grade school. I used fancy text lettering to print the menu items and costs and did a water color rendition of a wine bottle, candle, and plate of spaghetti for the cover. My friend, Bob, photocopied the inside text, attached the hand-painted cover to each of the seven menus, and laminated the completed menus. I was proud of my efforts and eager to show Tony.

The next night, after another entertaining day as a tourist in London, I brought the menus to Tony. He was delighted. And I got two weeks of free dinners—a tasty treat and a real boost to my limited funds. My calligraphy class from high school had helped me out—who would have known? And in high school, it was called Sign Painting.

I also befriended Miss Muriel Finch that fall. The following summer, Miss Finch gave me a gift. She said "I will let you live in my flat—a few blocks from Wysall Lodge—if you will wait on tables for breakfast five days a week." Of course, I would do it. It enabled me to come back to London for another three month vacation. Waiting on tables had always been a way for me to earn money between teaching jobs—or generally make some extra money. I was delighted that Miss Finch would let me do this. I had more to see in London, and this would give me the opportunity. Miss Finch was once again the maternal figure that would help take care of me. Miss Muriel Finch and Tony had shown me that I could depend on the kindness of strangers while traveling.

Miss Muriel Finch's English Breakfast

Ingredients:
2 eggs
3 pieces of bacon or link sausage
2 slices of white bread
Butter for toast
Some slices of fresh tomatoes

Directions:
Fry bacon or sausage. Blot grease and transfer to a dinner-size plate.

Fry eggs sunny side up in a medium skillet. Place next to breakfast meat on plate.

Toast white bread. Butter it and then slice it in half. Place toast in a toast holder which accommodates 4 halves.

Garnish with sliced tomatoes and serve.

Tony's Spaghetti and Meatballs

I created this recipe from my memory of Tony's meal.

Spaghetti Sauce
Ingredients:
1 medium onion, finely chopped (1 cup)
2 cloves garlic, crushed
1 t sugar
1 green pepper, finely chopped
1 t basil leaves
2 15-oz. cans tomato sauce
1 14-oz. can of tomato puree
1 l28-oz. can of whole tomatoes, mashed
1 c. chopped mushrooms
1 bay leaf
1 t oregano
grated parmesan cheese (for topping)

Directions:
Mix ingredients in a large pot. Simmer for 1½ hours, stirring occasionally. While sauce simmers, prepare meatballs (recipe below).

Meatballs
Ingredients:
1½ lbs. ground beef
¾ c. dry bread crumbs
1 egg
½ c. milk
1 medium onion, chopped

2 cloves garlic, crushed
1 T parsley, snipped
1 t. oregano
salt and pepper to taste

Directions:

Mix all ingredients together and form into 1 inch balls. Place in a large skillet with ¼ cup of vegetable oil. Cook for about 20 minutes, turning. Add to sauce and cook 30 minutes longer.

To serve, put a few meatballs and a small amount of sauce over spaghetti noodles of your choice on an individual plate, and mix sauce with the spaghetti.

Sprinkle with grated Parmesan cheese.

Recipes from My Friends While Working at St. Francis Hospital

Let me situate my teaching. I taught adolescents on the psychiatric unit of St. Francis Hospital in Pittsburgh, Pennsylvania—in the Lawrenceville section. In my classroom, I facilitated the examination of literature and the creation of original writing and art—all for self-expression and personal growth. I did this for seven years, and I loved it.

A child care staff member made this sign for me to have. I hung it in a frame in my room.

I eagerly awaited my classroom time with the students and enjoyed seeing them grow, develop, and improve because of high quality care in the school and in the hospital. But it was also a high stress position.

During the seven years I spent at St. Francis in the early and mid-1970s, I was my most physically active. I canoed and cross-country skied often during the seasons, exercised regularly several times a week at a spa, played racquetball once a week, and hiked from time to time. It was the most physically fit I'd ever been since my childhood. Physical activity was an excellent method of energy drainage for letting go of the strong emotional stress of the job.

- **Chris** was a person I spent a lot of time with as a colleague and friend. She was playful and fun to be with. We camped, canoed, and hiked during our five year relationship. Action was the word to describe our relationship. **Beef Stew** was a specialty of our camping experiences.

- **Sister Andre,** another colleague and friend, and I, also spent some time together camping and canoeing. As first year high school English teachers, we conversed at a diner for hours after teaching, trying to discern the best approaches to classroom dilemmas. **Sugar Roasted Pecans** tantalized us as we snacked during visits together.

- **Dianne**, yet another friend and colleague, and I, hiked, camped, cross-country-skied, and canoed together during this time. Her mother was also an orphan like I was, so her mother was very kind and invited me to their home for every holiday to share the meal and the evening with them. **Apricot Square Cookies** appealed to her need for the sweet and the practical Christmas cookie—they were made in a flash.

- **Ellie** mentored me during my time at St. Francis. She was my cerebral guide as well as affective guide for using story-making in the classroom. She encouraged me in every way to continue in my creative work and to continue with my education. But she also had me over to her home from time to time and fed me hearty soups and dishes. **Aunt Hattie's Chicken Recipe** is the one she includes here.

Delinquents: Chris

Camp Mer du Sault was set in a rather isolated pine forest in the mountains one hour north of Quebec City. It was cold there that summer—in the high 40s and low 50s. Occasionally, we had a sunny day in the 70s. Adventurous women, my friend Chris and I camped for four weeks there the summer of 1974. Even though the weather was cold and sometimes rainy, we had our rain gear to cope. We took my canoe and set up our tent on the edge of the river.

*Outside the tent, I had rain gear
for walking around the campsite.*

Chris and I had been friends for five years, and camped together every summer. We met teaching at Resurrection Grade School and became instant buddies. Spending a lot of time together hiking, eating out, seeing the humor and irony in things, talking about teaching, and man-hunting, we were like sisters—soul mates. This trip to Camp Mer du Sault was long planned and greatly anticipated. Although we camped every year, we usually went to Scarborough outside of Toronto so this was by far more adventurous, distant and remote than other years.

To cope with the cold nights, we unpacked the car and put our possessions in the tent. Then we put our air mattresses and sleeping bags in the rear of the car—the back seat was removed and left in Pittsburgh—and we slept with our feet facing the hatch door of my Volkswagen Rabbit—we were thin then. It was perfectly comfortable and warmer than the tent. In the morning, when we got ready to shower, we noticed that the shampoo kept in the tent had congealed overnight which made shampooing difficult.

After a hot shower, we needed a way to keep warm. I tried to make a fire in the grill provided which was not an easy task—I'm not sure why. I was usually pretty good at making a teepee fire but found it difficult to make one in a grill. Amazingly though, many men from Quebec were wandering around the campsite carrying a cup of coffee and conversing in shorts and short sleeve shirts. How hearty they were! They didn't seem to need a campfire. Dressed in turtlenecks, sweaters, and jackets, we were still cold. But when these men got near to help us build our fire, we discovered the smell of liquor on their breaths and in their cups. They might be hearty; but they were also numb.

The second evening after we arrived, Francois L'Heureux introduced himself to us as one of the camp workers. He was about our age and handsome, and came over when he saw us struggling to make another fire. He grabbed the paper out of my hand and wadded it up, put wood on top, lit it and a fire materialized. Chris and I were delighted—and grateful—and warm.

Francois then said in his good English with a French accent, "Stay here. I have just the thing for you."

He returned with a bottle of tequila, handed it to me and then pulled it back. "Do you have syphilis?"

Not debating how he thought syphilis was transmitted—you don't get syphilis from drinking out of the same bottle—I responded, "No," and he again handed me the bottle. I had a sip and passed it to Chris. She had a sip. We thanked Francois already feeling its warmth. Francois left but taught us two lessons—one about a fire building and one about keeping some tequila on hand for the cold nights. Later Francois showed us how to bank a fire so there would be hot embers the next morning from which to start the next day's fire. I was the fire builder and learned quickly.

During cold and rainy days, we often spent time in the Community Room with other like- minded campers. We stayed out of the weather, and I would read and Chris would sketch. We were not to be thwarted in our efforts to deal with the daily conditions no matter how uncomfortable they could be. But we had our midday reprieve—we went to a small French Canadian café just up the road for cups of coffee around three o'clock in the afternoon and enjoyed the warmth and the friendliness of the café and owner. In fact it was one day, August 9, 1974, that we saw a rerun of President Nixon waving good bye in front of Air

Force One, and the subtitles said that he had resigned. It did our hearts good to see this.

Another camping experience occurred one particular weekend during these four weeks. On a Friday afternoon, a group of six teenage boys accompanied by one young, male adult camped next to us. The kids drew attention as they paraded in carrying fishing rods and loudly punctuating every motion with a swear word. They could string their expletives in the most dramatic ways. After the kids put up a tent and settled in, the man, David, came over and explained that the teenagers were inner city kids—adjudicated delinquents. He worked with them and wanted to give them a chance to be in the woods and fish for trout. While dinner time seemed uneventful, later that evening, we could hear muttering and grumbling as they must have been going over their gear. At one point, I heard David exclaim, "What did you think? You could catch a whale with that hook."

The teens went to sleep at a reasonable hour, but we could hear David saying over and over on top of their chatter: "If you don't go to sleep, we won't go fishing in the morning." Finally, after what seemed hours—while Chris and I were enjoying a campfire and laughing—the tent next door settled into a quiet sleep. By this time, I had mastered building a big teepee fire, and we had learned to drinks some tequila to keep us warm too.

We never did hear them leave early the next morning to go fishing. Strutting into the campsite mid-morning, fish in hand, they were so proud. Under the guidance of David, they cooked the fish on the grill—

and there seemed to be much less swearing. They enjoyed eating the trout with great relish. While packing up to leave mid-afternoon, David came to tell us, "We caught more trout then we could eat, so I buried the left over fish wrapped in foil in a hole in the ground with ice packed around it." He showed us where and instructed us on how to grill it for dinner. David and these six young men soon left the campsite proud of the success of their fishing adventure. And Chris and I had a delicious dinner of fresh grilled trout that evening.

While they were trout fishing that morning, Chris and I had our own adventure taking out the canoe for a ride in the river. It was calm water so it was easy paddling. We enjoyed the trip talking away in the warm sun on an otherwise cool day.

We decided to have a contest to see who could swear the loudest. We each tried. Chris won.

Then we decided to have another contest to see who could scream the loudest. We both tried. I won.

Just then we turned a bend in the river and a young couple in a canoe passing us said, "Bon jour." We responded with an embarrassed, "Bon jour." Wouldn't you know, Chris and I would have this idea and get caught? So much for our attempt at being upstanding citizens—we were delinquents ourselves.

Beef Stew

Ingredients:
1 lb. stewing beef, cut up into 1" squares
1 c. sliced carrots
½ c. onion, finely chopped
8 small red potatoes, quartered
¼ c. celery
2 T cornstarch

Directions:
In a large pot, brown the stewing meat in oil.

Add water to cover meat and bring to a boil. Simmer for 1 hour.

Add onion, celery, carrots and potatoes. Cover with water and bring to a boil. Simmer for an additional hour or until everything is tender.

Thicken with cornstarch.

A Thirty-Something Adventure: Sister Andre

Nothing was unusual about driving my green Volkswagen Rabbit down the Pennsylvania Turnpike on the way to Towson, Maryland. I did this trip frequently. But, this time, my car sported a silver canoe on top. I thought it looked pretty slick. The canoe was mine, an Aerocraft—rated second only to Grumman. I was very proud that I had saved the money to buy it. I couldn't afford a Grumman, but my Aerocraft had high sides and good balance, cut nicely through the water and was perfect for me. On this sweltering Friday in mid-summer of 1978, the Susquehanna River was calling.

Getting ready for the trip down the Susquehanna River, the canoe sits on my VW Rabbit.

Sister Andre to others but just Andre to me—my good friend and colleague from Bishop Boyle High School joined me on the trip. In Towson, we would stay with another friend, Chris, who I also met as a teacher but at Resurrection Grade School. Andre and Chris had never met though both had heard of each other from me. I was the friend in common among us three. I had hiked and camped individually with both Chris and Andre. The three of us, in our 30s, viewed ourselves as rugged women and anxiously anticipated another outdoor adventure—this time canoeing down the Susquehanna.

We launched our adventure at 5:00 AM the next morning over a breakfast of oatmeal, eggs, bacon, toast and coffee. The cooler, packed with fruit, brownies, beverages, sandwiches for lunch—and sandwiches for dinner just in case our trip was longer than expected—was loaded into the car. We had calculated the canoe trip to last until two or three in the afternoon though I don't remember how many miles it was. Excitement grew as we began this journey.

As is typical of a trip down the river, we took two cars. At our final destination, we parked Chris's VW Bug. Then we drove back to our beginning point in my car. We removed the canoe—it took Andre and I together to lift it from atop the car—and put it near the edge of the water. The cooler, two paddles, and the life jackets were placed inside. Finally, we moved the car just off the bridge and parked it. Susquehanna River here we come!

I sat in the front of the canoe calling to guide the direction of the paddling, and Andre paddled in the rear. Thus, the quiet journey was occasionally punctuated by my vocalized "paddle to the left" or "paddle to the right." I paddled on my left and Andre paddled on her right. Chris sat in the middle, from her position around the food. Chris was the novice in the group although Andre and I weren't that much more experienced. Having never been on a river in a canoe before, we eagerly proceeded on this enterprising trip.

It was a beautiful sunny day. The riverside was lush with greenery at each bend. At one point, however, the river took a turn to the right, and before me, were about 20 cows spread out all over the hillside and spilling into the river. I yelled, "Paddle to the right!" Both Andre and I paddled to the right vigorously to get around the cows. They never bothered us—and they never seemed to be bothered by us. But they didn't look like they were going to move either. To us, it felt like a close call.

Taking note of the beauty on either side, we roamed through the winding Susquehanna River. The river was calm with a steady flow and an occasional small rock with white water. This is when we would "paddle to the right" or "paddle to the left." And our quiet and peaceful morning moved into lunchtime.

A tree limb on the bank invited me to grab hold so that we could pull ashore and tie up to it for lunch. As I grabbed the limb, I saw a bees nest there and yelled, "Paddle backward," as I flopped myself back on the seat, Chris and the cooler. Andre paddled us out before the bees even realized we were there. Relieved, we paddled on and looked for another tree limb, found one, tied up and enjoyed our sandwiches, fruit and beverage.

This was the life—and quite adventurous for us. It was our first river excursion.

We continued to paddle down the river, veering to the left or right, as small obstacles cut through the water. Then Chris asked if she could paddle. Andre and I agreed, and Chris proceeded to the front. Chris was doing well, when, all of a sudden we saw a huge rock to our right with white water all around. Chris did not warn us fast enough to clear the rock. Soon, we were sinking, and the canoe was being squeezed into the rock. All three of us were out of the canoe, but there was ground below our feet.

With as firm a footing as we could manage, we held on to the canoe and lifted the cooler and paddle to the top of the boulder. One paddle floated away. Then, we turned the canoe on its side and began lifting it—to the chant of "1-2-3 lift"—the adrenaline was flowing as we proceeded to remove the water a little at a time. Finally, we bailed out all of the water and lifted the canoe to the top of the rock. We were jubilant. We had succeeded and saved the canoe, one paddle and the cooler. The life jackets had saved us. We could manage with one paddle—people did that all the time. It was time to celebrate, so we sat on top of the boulder, broke out the brownies and ate ravenously.

We then carefully lowered the canoe down the other side, and, while Andre was holding on to it, Chris and I put in the cooler. Off again to finish the last part of our journey, we felt proud about overcoming such an obstacle. However, soon stress returned: we were near the time of finding our car, and we realized that we had forgotten to tie a cloth on the bridge to identify where the car was located. We came up to a bridge, discussed whether it looked familiar and concluded that it did. I climbed up the hill to check. Amazingly, our car was there. Loading things into the car and tying down the canoe followed. Now, relaxed enough to be hungry, we devoured our reserve sandwiches. But we were pleased that we had done so well—we had been successful on our first river canoe trip.

Eager to repeat our adventure, we bought a replacement paddle that night in order to do our adventure the next day. The next morning, however, we woke up exhausted and sore. We decided to stay at Chris's home and relax to coffee, bacon and eggs, the Sunday paper and to participate in conversation about our adventure. We were not quite the rugged women that we thought we were—but our spirits were adventurous. And I was reminded of the joy of friendship and camaraderie.

Brownies are the logical recipe to include here, but I must confess that we just used a box mix. So, I am including a festive recipe of Sister Andre's, Sugar Roasted Pecans. They are delicious but decadent too.

Sugar Roasted Pecans

Ingredients:
1 c. sugar
¾ t salt
½ t cinnamon
1 egg white
1 T water
1 lb. pecan halves

Directions:
Preheat oven to 250 degrees

In a bowl, mix salt, sugar and cinnamon and set aside

In a bowl, add egg white and water. Whip until a froth forms. Add pecans halves and stir around until pecans are covered.

Add egg-white-coated pecan halves to sugar and cinnamon mixture and coat the pecans again.

Spread coated pecans on a non-stick cookie sheet.

Bake 1 hour, stirring every 15 minutes.

A Christmas Gift: Dianne

Boxes of individual kinds of Christmas cookies lined one side of the stairway going up from Aunt Molly's main floor of the house to the attic. It was cool there, and the cookies, baked weeks in advance of Christmas, were kept fresh. Russian tea balls, spritz cookies, peanut butter cookies, sugar cookies, nut-filled cups, small fruit pastries and more lined these stairs. Our challenge as children was to sneak there and grab a cookie when we were free from Aunt Molly's eagle eyes guarding her cookies for Christmas.

Yes, I had fond memories of the Christmas cookie baking ritual but had never indulged in this ritual myself. At 30 years old, I made my first attempt with my friend Dianne, but it was a much more modest attempt. Our plan was to get together after work, eat dinner and bake three kinds of cookies. It was as simple as that—or so we thought. I wanted to do Russian tea balls, a favorite from my childhood, and Dianne wanted to make her favorite apricot squares. We both wanted to try gingerbread cookies. We came to my house with the necessary recipes and ingredients. I had the baking tools, bowls, and my baking ingredients set out on the kitchen table.

At 5:00 PM, we had dinner at a small table in the sun porch room. It was nearing sunset of what had been a rare sunny day in wintry Pittsburgh. We were surrounded by glass windows on all three sides with an apple tree out front. The declining sun was coming through the windows. It was a pleasant setting for our dinner of stuffed chicken breasts, roasted vegetables and dill potatoes. We accompanied the dinner with a moderately priced pino grigio. Dianne and I had met two years ago at a drama workshop and had since shared our love and joy of teaching with each other. Talking about the events of the day led to more personal conversation.

Then Dianne mentioned, "Since we're becoming good friends, I wanted you to know that I am gay. It's important that you know this about me."

I responded, "I appreciate your trusting me and being honest with me. It helps me understand you better. We are good friends, and that won't change."

A lengthy conversation ensued about her being gay as a teacher and her fear of being found out. This was taboo in 1975—still is in many places. The conversation drew us closer together. I felt compassion for this strong woman who was struggling with prejudice against alternative life styles. Life was difficult enough without people finding unimportant ways to make it more complicated. Conversation flowed easily over dinner and wine. We were on a friendship-high.

All of a sudden, it was 8:30 PM, and we had not yet begun to bake the cookies. So, we began. Slightly inebriated, we mixed the batter for the Russian tea balls. Just chopping the pecans into small pieces was labor-intensive and made this cookie time-consuming. While chopping and mixing, conversation continued interspersed with moments of laughter. We were getting silly. While this batter was chilling, we made the apricot squares. Dianne was the sensible one—she picked a simple cookie to bake. While they were baking, we mixed the gingerbread batter. At 9:30 PM, we called a colleague of mine to answer our question. Did we have the right consistency for her gingerbread dough? We did though it was thick and full of cracks.

Amazingly organized considering that it was later in the evening and after some wine, now, we were ready to take out the hardened Russian tea ball batter from the refrigerator and form it into balls to bake. At 10:30 PM, between talking and laughing, we had only rolled about 25 tea balls. Temporarily, we became more focused. We had just taken the apricot squares out of the oven to cool. Persistence was our mantra.

While the first batch of Russian tea balls baked, we cut the apricot into squares. Now, we pulled the Russian tea balls out of the oven and dusted them with powder sugar—their first layer of two layers of powdered sugar administered that night—and we put them aside. This cookie was never done. Like an assembly line, a new batch of Russian tea balls were formed and placed in the oven. Finally, at 11:30 PM, we were ready to roll out the gingerbread dough and cut it into cookie people—mama, papa and child. Surprisingly, the cracked, thick dough rolled out to a smooth brown consistency. We placed the gingerbread people on a cookie sheet and had them wait their turn to enter the oven.

Flour and powdered sugar flew around from time to time—on our faces, clothes, the table and the floor. Nevertheless, nothing could deter us from our mission. We had quite a system going. At 12:30 AM, out came the second batch of Russian tea balls to be dusted with powdered sugar. Finally, the gingerbread cookies could be baked. Out came the gingerbread cookies and in went the third batch of Russian tea balls. When the gingerbread cookies cooled, at 1:30 AM, we began decorating in our most artistic and colorful manner. It was a painstaking effort using small tubes of red, green and white frosting—not easy to control and maneuver. There were crooked smiles, even accidental frowns, crooked eyes, lopsided hair, clumsy shoes, irregular buttons down the body and more —and lots of silliness and laughter. We were giddy with exhaustion. Finally, the gingerbread cookies were decorated, and the Russian tea balls were dusted with powder sugar, twice. It had become a marathon—running against the clock to get done in time to get some sleep before work. So much for the joy of baking Christmas cookies.

At 3:00 AM, we were finished. We had tasted each batch of cookies after it had cooled. All of them were scrumptious, but—as the night went on—our stomachs grew sour from our being up so late, and, thus, we could not bear to taste the gingerbread cookies. However, everything was completely baked, cleaned up and packed up to store for a few weeks until Christmas. We would store them on the stairway to my attic. It would come to pass that they would be a hit for dessert following the Christmas dinner celebration—all except the gingerbread cookies that tasted terrible. We saved them for next year and shellacked them to hang as ornaments on the Christmas tree.

Yes, it was 3:00 AM, and Dianne and I would get up at 6:30 AM and, on three hours of sleep, teach a full day. Only at 30 years old could we do this. Ah, youth.

Apricot Squares

Ingredients:
1 c. dried apricots
1 8-oz. can crushed pineapples (not drained)
½ c. sugar
¾ c. margarine
1 c. sugar
1 c. flour
¾ t salt
½ t baking soda
½ c. chopped walnuts
1½ c. flaked coconut

Directions:
Preheat oven to 375 degrees.

Begin filling by simmering apricots and pineapple in pan for 20 minutes. Mix in ½ cup sugar and simmer for 5 more minutes.

Let stand.

Move to the crust by beating butter and sugar until light and fluffy. Stir together salt, flour and soda and add to creamed mix, gradually mixing well. Add chopped nuts and coconut.

Press 2/3 of crust mix (about 4 cups) in to bottom of a greased 9 x 13 pan.

Bake for 10 minutes and remove from oven.

Cool.

Spread filling over crust.

Crumble crust remains over top of filling.

Bake for 5 more minutes. Remove from oven.

Cool.

Serve in 1-½" squares.

Yield: About 50 cookies

Dedicated Teacher and Mentor: Ellie

My friend, Ellie

Ellie mentored me in the 70s and encouraged me to publish and get a PhD. Only 5% of women were getting this degree in the U.S. at that time.

It was 1973. Ellie was a dynamic woman as a drama therapist. She energized her audience of special education teachers as she had them do mime with partners in an evening workshop. She was insightful, informative and compelling as she spoke of the symbolic communication and the feelings expressed by students through drama activities. We teachers were enthralled with all of this.

Ellie was a vibrant, alive professor. She integrated theory and practice. She had times of interaction over drama therapy tools interspersed with insightful discussions. She was well-published and humbly included some of her articles as readings well situated with leaders in the field of drama therapy and psychodynamic theory.

Ellie was always encouraging to me. She suggested that I write a paper on my work in my classroom. She taught me how to think expansively—for me it was getting a PhD and in a field outside of education—in child development and child care. She stimulated thinking by introducing the Psychoanalytic Center and the Pittsburgh Association for the Arts in Education and Therapy. She always found time to be enthusiastic with students.

Ellie with two mentees of the 70s, Rosemarie and me

Ellie was a ground-breaker as she began the Pittsburgh Association for the Arts in Education and

Therapy, a professional association, and instituted the first Drama Therapy Conference. Ellie was honored by the Psychoanalytic Institute for her life time achievements. She is impressive in her work, competence and success. She inspires teachers.

Ellie is a nurturer in all that she does. One other way that she nurtures is through cooking. She explains why this is her special choice for a recipe to include here.

Aunt Hattie's Wonderful Chicken Recipe (aka "Turkey Tetrazzini")

Many years ago, as a novice cook, I was treated to Aunt Hattie's wonderful Chicken Recipe. Thereafter this became my no-fail dinner dish for family and friends. Many years and recipes later, I found an almost exact duplicate, called "Turkey Tettrazine," in an old cookbook. But chicken or turkey, to me, the dish will always be fondly remembered as "Aunt Hattie's Chicken Recipe." Easy, breezy.

Ingredients:
12-oz. package of spaghetti noodles, broken into 3-4" pieces
2 T olive oil
1 small onion, chopped
1 clove garlic, chopped
8 oz. mushrooms, sliced
1 red pepper (or small jar pimentos), diced
1-3 c. of shredded cooked chicken or turkey
1 14-oz. can mushroom soup
½ c. milk or cream

Directions:
Heat oven to 350 degrees. Grease a medium/large casserole dish.

Cook spaghetti as indicated on the package. Drain and set aside.

Meanwhile, in skillet, sauté onion in the olive oil until transparent but not browned. Add garlic, mushrooms, red pepper, and chicken.

Sauce 1:
Ingredients:
1 can mushroom sauce
½ c. milk or cream

Directions:
Add cream or milk to mushroom soup in a small sauce pan. Heat until nearly boiling.

OR Sauce 2:
Ingredients:
3 T butter
3 T flour
2 c. milk (or fat-free half-and-half)
¼ c. dry sherry (optional)
1 t. paprika

Directions:
Melt butter, stir in flour, and slowly stir in liquids and paprika.

Topping:
Ingredients:
½ c. Panko™ (bread crumbs)
2 T butter
2 T parmesan cheese

Directions:
Mix ingredients and heat lightly until butter melts.

To assemble the dish:

In greased casserole dish, mix drained spaghetti, chicken, vegetables, and sauce.

Top with bread crumb mixture.

Cook in 350 degree oven for 30 minutes or until top is brown (cover with foil if crumbs get brown too early).

If desired (I always did), serve with more sauce (mushroom soup or white sauce).

Friends for a Quarter of Century: Carlow University

Teaching at Carlow University was one of two best jobs I ever had—a good thing too since I held it for 22 years. From childhood, I always wanted to spend my time in the classroom. My love affair with school started in kindergarten; I had wanted to be a teacher ever since I was five-years-old. Throughout the many losses in my childhood, I felt cared for and attended to in school, so it was a good place for me to be. I attended every class anticipating challenge, fun, and even joy, and I was rarely disappointed. I was a successful learner and felt like I belonged. I did belong. Because I never really belonged in any one family, belonging in school meant a lot to me. Teachers were nurturing and nourishing—like the cherished mother I never had.

Teachers were life-embracing role models. That's what I wanted to be. Outstanding teachers knew their fields of knowledge and knew their learners.

Learners are active in the learning process; students are passive—and not what I experienced in school. Encouraging intellectual and academic success and supporting personal growth and development was their mantra. They smiled; they teased; and, they were serious about their subject. They seemed to genuinely enjoy what they were doing—teaching. Establishing an environment of psychological safety and trust was their strength. In this space, I thrived. I was an excellent learner and loved learning. I belonged in a classroom—that's where I wanted to spend my life—and did. I later was able to become this role model.

I had a great passion for the field of early childhood education. I believed in individualizing the lesson as much as possible. I established relationships with the learners and, when appropriate, got personally involved. I believed in and established a caring and challenging community of learners where everyone was valued and respected. I enjoyed the learners and the content and tried to share that. Ultimately, I wanted to nourish and nurture the independence and gifts of each learner. Outstanding teachers that I had had modeled this for me, and this is what I tried to be for my learners. Carlow afforded me this opportunity.

Carlow also presented me with many chances to be in leadership roles, and I loved those roles. I served on the Curriculum Committee and Faculty Senate for many years. In fact, I was chair of the Faculty Senate for five years. I actually learned about doing service projects during my tenure at Carlow. It was never emphasized to me previously. Carlow expected service to the university community and greater Pittsburgh

272

community. I did both and learned about the value and joy of it. It enriched my life.

The Carlow faculty members were very impressive. They were hard-working, dedicated, and committed to excelling in their fields. Working cooperatively, the faculty completed projects together. As I learned at Carlow, we accomplished so much more working together. Also empathetic and caring, the faculty were sensitive to the needs of their colleagues. I enjoyed working with my Carlow colleagues. Along with Sandie, Martha, and Dee of Oglebay fame, and Roberta from Piccolo Forno, Dick, Janice A., Clare, and Pat have continued to maintain friendships with me since my retirement. June was also a relationship from my Carlow era.

Simultaneously, I dealt with issues around Christmas. As I said, they were always evolving. When Eileen moved to West Lafayette, Indiana, for a while, my experience with the holiday and my sister evolved once more.

- In West Lafayette, Christmas became going to visit my family. **Eileen's Russian Tea Balls** were a holiday hit.

- **Dick** made the **Bœuf Burguignon** for me, and it was delicious especially because of the loving care involved.

- **Apple pie** is one of **Janice's** specialties although she is a Chef Extraordinaire.

- **Clare's** recipe for **Beulah's Tomato and Eggplant Pie** was a hit with her family at Christmas 2012.

- **Pat's** rendition of **Eve's Chili (for Rege)** tantalizes the appetite of chili lovers who prefer chili that is not highly seasoned.

- **June's** take on **Ellen's Hot Chicken Salad** was a specialty of the Elbow Room eatery and of my house. I often made it for Dick's dinner visits on Sundays.

A Family Christmas: Eileen

After several years of living together, Silvia, Eileen's roommate, decided to move to West Lafayette, Indiana, to get her PhD at Purdue University in Family and Marriage Counseling. Eileen and the kids moved with her. They shared a large sturdily-built split-level with two separate living spaces but a common living room, kitchen, and laundry. Stairs ran down from the kitchen to Silvia's quarters and up and off of the living room to Eileen and the kids' space. Painted a sunny yellow, it was inviting to all who entered.

Me, Lee-Ann, Anita, and Eileen enjoy breakfast of the porch in West Lafayette, Indiana.

The fenced-in yard was large and provided room for two, sweet, mature beagles, Max and Sammy, to roam from time to time during the day—and for Silvia and the kids to practice softball in as well.

They remained there for five years until Silvia finished the residency work on her degree. Then they returned to Florida, Gainesville this time, while she finished her dissertation. Silvia obtained a position in the counselor education program at the School of

Education at the University of Florida, Gainesville. Eileen could get a nursing job or nursing educator job just about anywhere, so Silvia took the lead on where they would live. Eileen was hired at Santa Fe Community College as a pediatric nurse educator. This time, Silvia and Eileen would live in separate houses—I think Silvia was ready to be more independent.

While they lived in West Lafayette, I made an eight-hour drive to visit and share every holiday with them—something Eileen and I treasured greatly. Over the years, Eileen and I had each come to learn how to enjoy the holidays from being with our friends—and that enabled us to know how to enjoy them with each other. While in West Lafayette, we also spent summers going to beaches like the Dunes near Chicago, ball games at Wrigley Field, a Cuban art museum, and restaurants like Bennigan's. These were fun times.

At Christmas time, I especially liked visiting—I finally had a family of my own to be with for Christmas. One year early on, I was so excited to join them for Christmas that I bought several sets of bubble lights for their Christmas tree—a very homey tradition. Another year, Eileen got Bingo set up for us to play on Christmas day. She bought and wrapped school supplies as prizes: notebooks, pencils, pencil sharpeners, and the like. Although I was resistant to playing Bingo, Eileen knew I'd play for school supplies, a favorite of mine, I guess because I was a teacher. I couldn't pass up new supplies.

I really missed Eileen when she moved back to Florida and we only saw each other once a year. I had come to count on her as my sister and my family for the holidays and summers. But we began talking on the phone every weekend for an hour or more. This was a very big concession for Eileen since she said, "I hate talking on the phone. I only do it because I know it is important to you for me to call." For me, I felt connected and good about these phone calls in the absence of her physical presence.

Russian Tea Balls (also called Mexican Wedding Cakes)

At Christmas time, Eileen, Lee Ann, Anita, and I always made Russian tea balls. We quadrupled the recipe and enjoyed them ourselves and with our guests.

Ingredients:
1 c. butter, softened
½ c. confectioners' sugar
1 t vanilla
2-¼ c. flour
¼ t salt
¾ c. finely chopped pecans
extra confectioners' sugar for rolling
red and green sprinkles (for Christmas)

Directions:
Heat oven to 400 degrees.

Mix thoroughly butter, sugar, and vanilla.

Work in flour, salt, and nuts until dough holds together.

Chill one hour before shaping dough into 1" balls. Place on ungreased baking sheet.

Bake 10-12 minutes or until set but not brown.

While warm, roll in confectioners' sugar.

Cool. Roll in sugar again. At Christmastime, roll in sprinkles the second time.

Yield: about 4 dozen cookies

Bonded: Dick

Dick embraces the arts and shares his love of them with his friends.

Dick encouraged, "You should attend the Fresh Start Program at Shadyside Hospital in order to quit smoking. Smoking is really bad for you, and Fresh Start is an excellent program." Dick and I met over this conversation in Franny's Café at Carlow University. I was a new faculty member, and he was an esteemed colleague.

Dick sometimes gave advice. He was a recent graduate of the Fresh Start Program and was not shy about making suggestions. I went although I did not have much faith in myself. I had tried to quit smoking on several occasions and knew how hard it was. But I was interested in dating Dick, so I tried.

Dick then further encouraged with "Why don't you join Smokers Anonymous as a support?" I attended a few meeting but was bored. Then Dick subtly let me know that he was gay, and that ended my interest in Smokers Anonymous. But the Fresh Start Program worked. I have not smoked a cigarette since. That budding friendship began over 25 years ago.

With gray hair, a darker mustache, and a kind face and eyes, Dick was a professor of art and art history at Carlow University. He was in his early 50s, and I was in my early 40s. Dick's vocabulary drew faculty note as he spoke or even just composed Faculty Assembly minutes. Faculty commented as they perused the minutes, "Let's see what Dick has to say in the minutes today." He had the admiration of the faculty for this. I enjoyed learning words like "convivial" and "*au courant*," for example. Dick could cite the lovely imagery in Proust novels. Well educated, brilliant, Dick was an oil painter by vocation and avocation, painting photo realistic works as well as surrealistic ones. He is a Renaissance man. As a professor, he could have taught anything in the humanities and was especially accomplished in the arts.

He is thoughtful, insightful, funny, and wise. The afternoon that I moved in to my new house in Shadyside, he bicycled over to welcome me to the neighborhood. We often had discussions about our childhoods, and he shared helpful insights and reflections about my losses and neo-Dickensian adolescence. I enjoyed and appreciated the stories of his very well–cared-for childhood and doting parents. And we laughed a lot about many humorous and not-so-humorous things. We could also be witty about the turns that life had taken for each of us.

Dick spent ten more years at Carlow before he retired. And we spent Thursday and Sunday evenings together. We were an unlikely twosome—he the intellectual and me the intuitive type. On Thursdays, early on, we would meet at the Elbow Room at 9:00 PM for dinner; and in later years, we would meet at Max and Erma's, both in Shadyside. We would sit and talk about recovery, for he was in AA and I was in a Recovery International for people with emotional issues.

Dick and I always enjoyed stimulating coffee and equally stimulating conversation.

Over dinner, Dick's treat, we had lively conversations about the arts, books, life, Carlow—any topic was up for discussion. We were interesting storytellers, and we each had numerous stories to tell.

On Sunday nights, he came to my house for dinner. I cooked—sometimes a hot chicken salad with fresh greens and oven-baked French fries or an old family recipe of Hungarian chicken paprikash with egg dumplings. Although I was a pretty perfunctory cook for myself, when I cooked for others, I enjoyed the cooking. We continued conversing and storytelling over food and beyond. We often walked around Morningside or Shadyside where I lived. We followed up sometimes by listening to the operas on WQED public radio. Dick, being quite an expert in opera, added enriching commentary that I enjoyed. We spent the last few years before he retired writing our memoirs. On Sunday evenings, we read our memoirs to each other—as we progressed in creating them during the week. Dick's writings were filled with extended, lush description ripe for visualization. My writings were straight and to the point, brief statements of fact. We were each other's devoted audience, and I loved it.

Dick once came over for Thanksgiving, and we cooked a Thanksgiving meal together. I don't remember what we had besides the turkey, but I remember thinking it was quite delicious. But an interesting thing happened. After Dick carved the turkey at the table, and we both sat down and began to eat, Dick asked, "Could you remove the carcass? It is aesthetically offensive." I had never thought of it before, but it was. Dick was always the artist. His whole life and every aspect of it were focused around issues of aesthetics.

After ten years, Dick retired and moved to San Francisco. It was very difficult for me to say goodbye to such a dear friend. It was not without lengthy crying and painful sadness. I was losing a close friend to a great distance. It was another significant loss in my life. Of course our relationship would change. We continued with lengthy emails each night talking about the day's experiences for about two years. Then Dick met a partner, and our emails became much less frequent. During our emailing, I met someone too.

Even though we email much less frequently, we do keep in touch and count on one another to share our joys and insights with each other. Dick is a very compassionate and sympathetic listener when I really need it, and he always gives wise counsel. I like to think that I do the same.

Dick has changed from pursuing painting to pursuing writing. In the last few years, he has been working on a series of three historical fictions set in medieval times. Although I am reading memoirs and autobiographies exclusively at this time, Dick asked if I would read his first book, and I agreed—after all, this is what friends do. I read the first one, which was impressive, engaging, actually, compelling. I then asked to read the second one. Dick has also asked to read my stories. So we have renewed our friendship with writing again—ten years later. We are again listening to each other's stories.

Dick is amazing. At 65-plus, he has gotten his first of a trilogy of books accepted for publication by a British company, Knox Robinson Press. He has signed a contract for the first of his three historical fiction novels. He could have signed for all three, but he didn't want to wait until the third one was completely written and accepted. So his first book is being published in early 2015. How terrific! I celebrate in his joy.

Close friends mean a lot to me. Over the 50 years since I left Cleveland for Pittsburgh, I have built a family of friends. I cherish them and depend on them for support and joy. Dick is that kind of friend. He is a champion of my ability to overcome strife and make a good life for myself. I appreciate that.

Bœuf Bourguignon

Dick once made a delicious Bœuf Bourguignon for me—a recipe from Phil, a Carlow colleague who lived in France after World War II.

Ingredients:
1 lb. beef tenderloin, cubed
butter or olive oil for sautéing
1 c. beef stock
2 cloves garlic, minced
1-½ cups red wine, burgundy
1 medium onion, chopped
2-3 whole carrots, sliced
1 t thyme (crucial)
1 t sage
2 or 3 bay leaves
12 white mushrooms, chopped
wide flat noodles

Directions:
Using butter or oil, sauté carrots, onions, and mushrooms in a large frying pan with a lid. Remove from pan and set aside.

In the same pan, add more butter or oil and sauté finely chopped garlic and chunks of beef until browned.

Add beef stock, thyme, sage, and bay leaves. Let simmer on low for 20 minutes, adding a very small amount of flour in water when needed to thicken the gravy (if desired).

Separately, cook wide flat noodles according to directions on package.

Gradually add to stock, burgundy, and then onions, mushroom and carrots. Let simmer another 10 minutes.

Serve over noodles and enjoy.

A Helping Hand: Janice A.

Janice eagerly shares her knowledge of teaching with her friends and colleagues.

Janice is a good and gentle person, who is always kind. I have known her for over 20 years and met her in the School of Education at Carlow University, where she has been chairperson in elementary education and then middle school education for the last fifteen or so years. She is a hard worker and a dedicated teacher. She always puts others ahead of herself. She will help anyone that she can. She believes in the Christian tradition and lives it out as I see it, but she does not proselytize.

Janice was a trusted and valued colleague over my years at Carlow. When I was teaching, Janice and I spent a lot of time discussing reading and language arts, her field, and story-writing, my field. We would discuss the commonalities and differences in our fields and our approaches to teaching. Actually, our classroom model for teaching was the same. We both facilitated the learning rather than lectured. We both provided hands-on, active learning, and we both used a lot of cooperative group classroom activity. If you looked in on either of our classes, there was a hum of conversation as each group of three or four students worked together on a project. Janice and I would be moving around the room as resources when needed. From time to time, students would present their small group projects to the class. We both loved teaching and talking about it.

Janice has been a reliable and caring friend over the years. One time, during a semester, when my psychiatrist could not find an effective anti-depressant for me right away, I spent several weeks struggling with teaching one class. I had trouble focusing and sustaining my energy. Weekly, Janice would sit down with me and talk me through my lesson plan and ideas. Always kind, Janice asked, "What will you do in class today?" She listened patiently as I described my approach to that day's class. Also, when I was teaching about children with learning disabilities, for example, Janice responded with, "Here is a book of case studies to examine. You could then present some case studies." Thus, I could involve the class in hands-on, active learning. Janice did this as a supportive friend and without judgment.

Even though I retired three years ago, we continue to maintain our friendship. We meet monthly at Panera's on the Boulevard of the Allies for extended lunches and good conversations. Janice gets a salad and half of a turkey panini, and I get a bowl of chicken noodle soup and a baguette. We lean into each other and confide as we talk about teaching, my Osher classes, our friends, our families, and Carlow. All of a sudden, three hours have passed.

Janice is a wonderful cook. She is famous for her spaghetti and homemade sauce and meatballs. She also bakes delicious bread. But another item she produces in her kitchen is her delicious apple pie, which she has chosen to include here.

Apple Pie

Pie Crust:
Ingredients:
2-2/3 c. all-purpose flour
½ t salt
1 c. vegetable shortening
7 t. ice-cold water
1stick (½ c.) butter, softened

Directions:

In large bowl, mix flour and salt: Cut in shortening with pastry cutter, or by crisscrossing two knives. Cut and blend until dough is in pea-sized balls.

Special tip: Mix in ice-cold water into contents of small bowl with fork until all is well-blended. The key to a flaky crust is to make sure you don't overwork the dough. Pie crust is not bread dough. If you overwork it, it will be tough.

Divide the dough into 2 balls: Using hands, form dough into balls. One will be used for the bottom, and the other will be the top.

Roll one ball out on paper or cloth, rolling from the center out so dough is about 1/8-inch thick. If using a pastry board, applying more flour and flipping the dough helps.

Carefully place the dough into a 9-inch pie pan: Gently press it into the pan. Use a sharp knife to trim the edges.

Fill your pie with the apple mixture. Add 2-3 pats of butter on top.

Apple Mixture:
Ingredients:
8 c. cooking apples, pared, cored, quartered, sliced thin
1/3 c. light brown sugar, firmly packed
1/3 c. granulated sugar
1 T cornstarch
4 t ground cinnamon
¼ t ground nutmeg
¼ t salt
2 T butter
A saucer of milk (for top crust)
Approximately 1 T sugar (for top crust)

Directions:
Preheat oven to 425 degrees.

In a small bowl, mix sugars, cornstarch, cinnamon, nutmeg, and salt.

Place apples in a large bowl and sprinkle sugar mixture over apples. Toss gently and let stand for ten minutes or until a little juice forms.

Place apple mixture into the bottom pastry.

Moisten overhanging edge of bottom pastry before placing top pastry and trimming overhang to one inch. Press overhanging edges, turning under, to seal them together around the edge of the pie. Then pinch edge to stand up and finish with fluted edges (optional).

Place the top pastry over the apple mixture.

With a sharp paring knife, cut decorative slits on the top of the pastry to allow steam to escape. If you want a crispy top, brush top of pastry with a little milk and sprinkle with some sugar.

Place pie in preheated oven and bake 40 minutes. Pie is ready when apples are tender and juice bubbles through slits of top crust. Watch to make sure that the edge of the crust does not brown too early. Cover edges of crust with narrow strips of foil if necessary.

Discussions around Soufflés: Clare

Clare listening and conversing—what she does so well

Coffee. Mini soufflés. Breakfast together at Panera's on the Boulevard of the Allies near Carlow University. Clare and I meet occasionally but importantly to keep in touch. She is a busy administrator, Dean of the School of Nursing at Carlow. The program is large and complex, and she leads it well. She is hard-working and dedicated, and one of the most esteemed faculty members at Carlow. I am honored to continue in this friendship with her. Even though I am no longer at Carlow full time, I enjoy hearing about her program and the ongoing challenges of nursing in higher education today.

Over the years, everyone at Carlow has come to know Clare as a leader. She has held just about every leadership position from chair of the Faculty Senate to chair of the mission committee for Middle States review. She leads wisely and democratically and is respectful of each member's contribution.

Besides being an outstanding leader, Clare is a warm and caring person whom I have known for 25 years. Like me, she's a talker. Yet she is also a good listener and discussant, and we have some lively conversations together. We talk about my Osher Life Long Learning classes, her work, my memoir life story writing group, her work, my interest in cooking, and her work—it reminds me of why I retired from Carlow.

Clare and I have intense and sometimes light-hearted, two-hour dialogues about our current lives. We both like to punctuate serious conversation with ongoing humor and irony. We have far-reaching political discussions while eating delicious soufflé.

We talk about topics such as the current state of the Catholic Church, the experiences each of us had in grade school and high school, Catholic education, issues around Planned Parenthood, President Obama and racism, health care today, mental health issues and spirituality as well as the challenges of everyday life. She is quite empathetic as I speak of my personal dilemmas. She is a psychiatric nurse by trade, and her sensitivity in responding to the soul of the other is apparent. I'd like to think that I do the same for her.

Clare also shares with me her interesting and impressive ongoing project on spirituality and cancer patients that she has been working on for years with a research team from the University of Pittsburgh. This research was an outgrowth of her last sabbatical.

Clare is a kindhearted yet private person. On a personal note, she always finds the time to fit in a conversation with another person. She listens well and responds caringly. Although Clare is one of the most high-powered professionals I know, she is also one of the most compassionate persons too.

Beulah's Tomato and Eggplant Pie

Clare's recipe originates with Susan Wittig Albert's mystery series, The Darling Dahlias.

Ingredients:

1 small eggplant, peeled & sliced thin
1 large tomato, sliced ¼-inch thick
½ large onion, sliced thin
melted butter (or olive oil)
1 T finely chopped fresh basil
½ t dried oregano
½ t dried thyme
½ t dried summer savory (sage can substitute)
pepper
crust for a 9-inch pie, unbaked
¼ c. grated yellow cheese (I used Asiago)
3 eggs, unbeaten
¼ c. milk
1 t prepared mustard

Directions:

Rinse both sides of eggplant slices thoroughly (note: some folks salt both sides & let sit for 15 minutes first. It isn't necessary to decrease any bitterness. Just rinsing thoroughly achieves the same effect). Pat dry.

Brush both sides of the eggplant, tomato, and onion slices with the melted butter or olive oil.

Arrange eggplant on a cookie sheet, leaving space for the tomatoes & onions.

Bake at 350 degrees for 10 minutes.

Remove from oven. Add the tomatoes and onions. Sprinkle with herbs and pepper. Return to oven until lightly browned.

Remove and cool slightly. Layer the eggplant slices on the pie crust.

Set aside a few tablespoons of cheese for later. Cover the eggplant slices with the remaining cheese, tomato, and onion slices.

In a separate bowl, mix the eggs, milk, and mustard. Pour the mixture over the slices in the pie crust.

Sprinkle the top with the remaining cheese.

Bake at 350°F until the egg/milk mixture is firm (about 35-40 minutes).

Living Life Intentionally: Pat

*Pat is serious-minded about education, yet she has a
wonderful sense of humor and enjoys life.*

Funny. Dramatic. Intelligent. Creative. Spontaneous.
Reflective. Sensitive. Caring. Pat was my next door
neighbor at Carlow University where she was the
director of the secondary education program at the
time. Her office door was always open, and she was

busy either meeting with a student or typing up documents necessary for her work. But she would find the time to stop and visit with me when I walked by and popped my head in the door.

Pat always dressed to the nines at work. She wore the most fashionable outfits. It was interesting to observe what she was wearing. She was a former high school English teacher, and, I am sure, as such, she drew the attention of the young women in her classes because of her wonderful wardrobe. Because she relates to people so caringly and intently, her clothing never interfered with her building a relationship with each young woman in her class.

As a high school English teacher, I am also sure that she drew the attention of her young students because of her sense of drama. She must have made the works of literature come alive through her dramatic interpretations. I could hear and see her read her students excerpts from Shakespeare's *The Merchant of Venice* in a most lively and powerful voice so that all of the youngsters would understand how Shylock is a human being who bleeds like all of us.

On a lighter note, Pat is just as dramatic singing with a friend at a party at Carlow or at a local bar. They sing and dramatize "Aquarius," from the now classic musical, *Hair*. "As the moon enters the seventh hour," the two of them emote, engaging their audience in active listening if not song too.

Pat is always very welcoming and enthusiastic when she sees someone she knows and likes. She warmly smiles and dramatically announces her happiness at seeing the person. So whenever I stop up to the School of Education at Carlow to sign off on a master's thesis—now that I am retired, I am no longer present on a daily basis—and I run into Pat, I can enjoy her exclamation, "Ellen, it is so good to see you. I really miss you. How are you?" Pat is intent, focused, and dramatic as she poses this question. I feel happy to be in her presence, receiving her attention. I feel very important to her.

Pat is so bright. She was a delight to work with as a colleague in the School of Education because she entertained insightful, reflective questions and comments on all topics related to learning, especially the learning of college students. Although we each directed our own programs, hers in secondary education and mine in early childhood education, we shared the commitment to intentionality in quality learning of college students as well as to children and adolescents.

Pat is deeply committed to all that she does. She has a focus and intentionality in saying, "hello," to me as well as to teaching and to the learning process. She lives life intentionally.

Eve's Chili (for Rege)

Pat writes, "To accommodate my father's conservative Irish palate, my Italian mother created a chili recipe that has no spicy kick to it. It is a mild, flavorful blend of delicious tastes, and it is perfect to serve on a cold winter afternoon or evening. I like it plain but have also paired it with rice or noodles. My mother usually served it with ground beef, but I prefer ground turkey. Either will do. This is an easy recipe that you can make quickly. ... Incidentally, a picture of my mother and father on their wedding day is in the photo. If you look on the shelf behind and below me, you may be able to see them at the altar."

Ingredients:
1 lb. all natural fresh ground turkey (94% lean, 6% fat) or beef

1 c. water + 30 oz. water (2 refills of the spaghetti sauce can at different points in the recipe)

1 large onion, chopped

2 15-oz. cans of plain spaghetti sauce (I like Contadina because it's relatively low in sodium—280 mg.)

1 15-oz. can of kidney beans, drained and rinsed

Directions:
Place turkey and water in a large sauce pot (8 qts. if you double this recipe, a little smaller if you don't). Stir and cook over low heat.

When almost all the water has been absorbed, add chopped onion and mix.

When all moisture has been completely absorbed, add one can of spaghetti sauce and one can of water. Stir. Add the other can of spaghetti sauce, then another can of water. Add beans and stir.

Cover and cook over a medium-low heat for at least an hour. If you cook these ingredients longer than one hour, and I highly recommend that you do (I've let it cook at times for up to six hours), be sure to lower the heat to a simmer. The longer the ingredients simmer, the thicker the chili becomes, and the better it tastes. This chili is even better tasting the following day.

Yield: four average-sized soup bowls.

Follow That Car!: June

In the late 1990s, on a sunny, crisp fall day, I was at June's house in Mt. Lebanon. In her late 60s, June was white haired and rosy complexioned. June had just retired from teaching and directing the master's program in early childhood education at Carlow University. We had met five years earlier as faculty in the School of Education when I was director and faculty in the undergraduate program in early childhood education. We had done some independent co-consulting together along with teaching and directing while in the same school. This fall day, we were meeting in order to work on a presentation for a conference on play and children. When we decided to break for lunch, June suggested a restaurant that I did not know in the South Hills, but I agreed to follow her and meet her there. I was always up for trying a new restaurant with superb food—one of my favorite pastimes. We would take separate cars since each of us had our own engagements after lunch.

I waited outside June's garage for her to pull out, so that I could follow her to the eatery. She led in her silver car, and I followed up and down the streets in Mt. Lebanon. It's a good thing that I was following because I had no idea where we were or where we were going. We went around bends and curves, through stop signs and lighted intersections, and across roads. I kept following. As we continued driving, I grew hungrier and hungrier. Finally she pulled up at a house. I guessed that she had a quick errand to run. I pulled over behind her, and the car door opened. Out of the silver car stepped—a man! Where was June? Where was June's car? Where was I?

This was the era of no cell phones and GPSs as common car apparatus, so what could I do? I got out of the car and ran up behind the man. I told him that I was lost. I neglected to mention that I had been following him. He was about six feet tall and slender with dark black hair and blue eyes. He was very handsome. And I was unmarried. I asked, "Excuse me, could you tell me how to get to Washington Road?" He did. From there I could navigate home. Unfortunately I had an appointment that required that I proceed back to the Parkway East immediately—no time to flirt. You know the potential traffic jams on the parkway.

Since we both had commitments afterward, June and I did not have time to reconvene at her house and try a second time to go out to lunch.

From Washington Road, I found my way back to the east side of town, which was familiar to me. I realized that I was still hungry, so I treated myself to lunch at the Elbow Room in Shadyside. They serve a wonderful Hot Chicken Salad, which I accompanied with a glass of merlot. And, of course, I spent some time wondering what it might have been like to flirt with the man with the watery blue eyes whom I followed in the silver car. Oh well. Life goes on. Now I was ready to face my semi-annual check-up with my doctor well-fortified—and with an unplanned adventure too.

I talked to June on the phone later that day. June asked, "What happened to you?" and I explained. She told me that she had waited a while and then had proceeded to have lunch too. We had a good laugh. I told her that I had found a new way to meet a man.

Ellen's Hot Chicken Salad

I have a version of Hot Chicken Salad that has baked fries rather than French fries and, thus, is healthier but tastes as good. This recipe also uses healthy olive oil.

Ingredients:
4 c. baby spinach leaves
1 small baking potato, peeled
1 chicken breast
3 T part skim shredded cheddar
1 small onion, sliced
10 cherry tomatoes
2 T olive oil
olive oil cooking spray
2 T light ranch salad dressing

Directions:
Cut chicken into 1 inch cubes, brown in oil, and cook thoroughly. Set aside.

Caramelize onion slices in oil. Set aside.

Slice potato into thin wedges Place on non-stick cookie sheet. Spray with oil and sprinkle with salt. Bake for 20 minutes on each side or until golden. Set aside.

On a plate, layer salad mix, caramelized onions, shredded cheese, tomatoes, potatoes, and chicken.

Place light ranch in a container on the side.

DESSERT

The treat. The promise of more friendships to come.

New Friends

Anticipation is the key word in making a new friend. What will the relationship hold? How demanding will it be? How rewarding will it be? What will be the joys of it? Every potential new friend holds new possibilities for relating. Will it involve lengthy talks on the phone, extended/frequent emails, visits over coffee or tea, gatherings over dinner, meetings at a home? Anticipating all of this and seeing what evolves is the stuff of potential new friendships.

- **Elizabeth** presents a healthy **Haluski** (the bane of my childhood but now a delight to me).

- **Win's Lemon Meringue Pie** gets rave reviews from garden club and church.

- **Sharon L.'s Fiery Italian Stir Fry** uses any and all ingredients found in the fridge at any one time.

- **Sharon's Mushroom and Broccoli Stir-fry**, a healthy and delicious dish, shares her Chinese culture with us.

- **Keith's Molasses Crinkle** cookies top off any meal or please us as a treat at any time.

- **Marsha's Saturday Morning Scones** tantalize our taste buds anytime.

- **Veronica's Sweet Potatoes á là Debbi** is a holiday delight.

- **Joanne's Beef Oriental** is simple but tasty and a quick meal solution.

- **Barb's Strawberry Cream Pretzel Dessert** delights us visually and in our taste buds. It is just plain fun to have and eat.

Over a Pot of Tea: Elizabeth

Elizabeth with her cosmopolitan family is creative and entrepreneurial in her writing endeavors.

Every other Tuesday, from 1:00 PM to 3:00 PM, you can find Elizabeth and me at King's on Golden Mile Highway in Plum Borough. We are becoming friends and are a writing support group with an *n* of two. We begin by ordering, usually soup and a pot of tea. The wait staff knows us well from the frequency of our visits, the duration of our stays, and our generous tips. Frequently Elizabeth chooses a cup of cream of potato soup. I select a bowl of vegetable beef soup, and we receive our own pot of tea. Then we proceed to catch up on our busy lives.

Elizabeth has three blogs, a life story writing group in Plum Library, and is involved in trying to start several other life story writing groups. But most importantly, in terms of her writing, Elizabeth is an author who has published two books, *What My Mother Didn't Know* and *Dancing in the Rain*. Her books humorously examine poignant and simple aspects of family life. She is full of energy and enthusiasm for writing—actually, for life in general. She is a dynamo. Amazingly, she is also the mother of two young children.

We also meet to share one writing each—a draft of a work in progress that we want the other's input on. We take turns reading a story out loud and then discussing the writing. Elizabeth is very fine at the technicalities of writing as well as the conceptual components, so she generously and gently critiques my writings, usually asking questions, which assist me in making them more detailed. Elizabeth believes that if a writer is not challenged to take the next step, she will remain stuck on the same level—thus, Elizabeth's helpful input. I am an amateur writer, writing purely for the pleasure of writing. Elizabeth is a skilled writer. I listen to her read her stories with great admiration and raise an occasional, critical question for clarity or detail. We are very helpful to each other.

Elizabeth is an artist, who frequently sees the humor in life and expresses it in her writing. Her story, for example, about her sister and her saving chewing gum for later use on the underneath of a dresser drawer demonstrates their childishly literal translation of their mother's directive to not waste gum insufficiently chewed. The story is beautifully written, hilarious, and shows Elizabeth's skillful art form.

Though Elizabeth is a brilliant writer, her most outstanding trait to me is her willingness to be helpful to someone else. I have observed this over and over in her and find it impressive. Whether through a book, a blog, a personal relationship, a life story writing group, Elizabeth is always ready to assist others. She did a Share a Pair community activity in Plum Borough. Here, participants paired up according to the theme of a serious or a humorous story. The partners were proud to have their writings published online. Now Elizabeth has published a hard copy book of the writings. Yes, Elizabeth helps others—and she likes to do that—and we benefit from her giving.

Haluski

Elizabeth presents a modified, healthy recipe for Haluski. It is a version of my childhood cabbage and noodles that I now love.

Ingredients:
½ 16-oz package egg noodles
3 cloves of garlic, crushed
½ medium yellow onion, sliced
1/3 head cabbage, cut in strips about 1" x 2.5"
1-½ t butter or margarine
1-½ t olive oil
¼ t salt
black pepper to taste

Directions:
Prepare noodles as directed on package. Set aside.

Steam the cabbage in a steamer for 7-10 minutes. Remove and set aside.

Melt butter or margarine with olive oil in a large frying pan or wok on medium high heat. Add sliced onions and a sprinkling of salt. When the onions begin to turn clear around the edges, add the garlic. After a few minutes, add the cabbage. After a few minutes, add the cabbage and noodles. Add the remaining salt.

Continue to sauté until the onions begin to brown.

Serve hot.

Yield: Makes 6 ½-cup servings.

My Eighty-Something Friend: Win

Win enjoys feeding this kangaroo as others look on.
She loves animals and will get to each one.

I own a stunning charcoal drawing of an Argentinean gaucho which hangs in my living room over one of my couches. The 18" x 24", framed sketch of the gaucho reveals his weathered face, a bandanna around his neck, a hat, and intense eyes. This drawing was once part of an art exhibit by Win at the Monroeville Library. It is powerful and impressive. Although one of her prize possessions, Win has chosen to give it to me. I was once visiting her at her home and looking at all of her wonderful, skillfully done art work from the exhibit, and I admired the sketch. Win gave it to me. I am honored.

Win is my eighty-something friend. I met her at my life story writing group in Monroeville. Although she says that she has completed the writing of her life's stories, she continues to come to the group faithfully because it is the one of the "highpoints" of her month. Her comments and insights during the group about others' writings show the wisdom someone her age may have—and she has it. She has let me read her life stories, and they have shown her to be a talented writer and a strong woman who is a survivor despite much adversity.

Currently, Win is in great pain from her vertebrae in her back. They are crushed together and create noticeable discomfort in her as shown through her facial expressions and body movements. Yet she persists in getting around, doing what needs to be done. She cares for her aging dog, Max, her buddy and daily companion. He himself has "issues," so Win thinks they're a perfect match. Max keeps Win out and about daily as she takes Max for his several walks.

Quite the independent woman, Win takes herself on outings from time to time. She will go to see a movie that interests her and then take herself out for a steak dinner at Max and Erma's. If no one is available, it does not deter her. She proceeds on her own.

Win's life story also demonstrates two wonderful experiences that she had. One was her art exhibit at the Monroeville Library. Her paintings and a few charcoals are stunning portraits from photographs that she herself took. Win's second spectacular experience was her photo safari to Africa—a life time dream of hers. You can hear the delight in her voice as she retells the story of each of these two events.

Win loves Betsy Ann's chocolate covered cherry cordials. She is a delight to watch as she opens the bag and discovers the prize. "My favorites!" she exclaims as she puts them away for a special time when she will treat herself to one. They are to be savored.

Win and I have the best phone conversations. We talk about religion—she herself is a practicing Christian but does not proselytize. We discuss politics, the military retuning home, legalization of prostitution, the legalization of drugs, and more. No topic is off limits. She is honest, open, and interesting to converse with, and I look forward to these occasions. Win is a new friend whom I just made over the last three years through my life story writing group.

Lemon Meringue Pie*

People in Win's church and garden club say of Win that on her tombstone will read, "She made a hell of a lemon pie!" so she is including the recipe here.

Ingredients:
4 T ARGO Corn Starch
1 c. sugar
5 T lemon juice
¼ t salt
2 T margarine
3 eggs, separated
1-½ t grated lemon rind
1-½ c water
1 (9-inch) pre-baked pie shell
6 T sugar

Directions:
Mix corn starch, salt, and ½ cup of sugar in the top of a double boiler.

Slowly stir in water.

Stir constantly in the double boiler until mixture thickens. Cover and cook 10 minutes.

Beat egg yolks slightly and mix with ½ cup sugar.

Stir in small amount of hot mixture. Immediately after, stir back into remaining hot mixture.

Stir 10 minutes more.

Remove from heat; gently stir in margarine, lemon rind and juice.

Cool. Pour into pie shell.

Meringue:
Directions:
Beat egg whites to soft peaks.

Beat 6 T of sugar, one at a time.

Beat mixture to stiff peaks.

Pour meringue over the mixture in the pie crust, sealing it to edge of crust.

Bake at 325 degrees for 15-20 minutes or until lightly browned.

Cool at room temperature.

*Adapted from recipe on ARGO Corn Starch, Foods Company, Memphis, Tennessee.

Kind—with a Dash of Energy and Fire: Sharon

Sharon facilitates our life story writing group with loving care and compassion as well as solid guidance.

A woman tries to place a covering over an art portfolio. Other students walk by not really noticing as they move on to sit for lunch or to exit the building into the downpour. Sharon L. is sitting in the general vicinity. She goes over to the woman and softly asks, "Can I help you cover the portfolio?" It is pouring down rain and people are getting drenched. The girl is struggling to place a black garbage bag over the portfolio. Now, Sharon and she are negotiating together and succeed at covering the portfolio with the garbage bag. The woman thanks Sharon and walks out into the torrents of rain with a firm hand gripping the covered portfolio. Sharon resumes her seat with me at the table to sip her water and visit over lunch and before our class, "Self-Publishing on a Shoestring." Sharon is teaching this class in the Osher Life Long Learning Program at the University of Pittsburgh.

Sharon distributes a class roster so that students can be in touch with each other if we want to. Thus, we can connect beyond the classroom to offer support, encouragement, and motivation to each other as we proceed with the self-publishing process. Sharon encourages us to consider this option after class ends.

Nancy from our life story writing group has lost her car keys in the library bathroom. A woman has accidentally picked up the keys and taken them home with her from the library thinking they were her own keys. The woman lives a 10 minute drive away from the library. Sharon offers to drive Nancy to the woman's house to get the keys, and to drive Nancy back to the library to pick up her car. Sharon does this without any fuss or fanfare.

Sharon tells me, "Rich needs a reader for a draft of a part of a book he is writing." Rich then continues the conversation. "The book will be about helping hospice patients write their memoirs. Would you be interested in helping me by reading a draft of 20 or so pages?" Sharon has connected two people of similar interests who can be a support for and help to each other.

Sharon performs acts of kindness quietly in a day that could go unnoticed to the undiscerning eye. She slips them into her day in a gentle way. All around her benefit from this—as a direct recipient or as a role model.

This is the same Sharon Lippincott who is author of *The Heart and Craft of Lifestory Writing* and two memoirs, who writes The Heart and Craft of Life Writing, a weekly blog on writing, and who facilitates a bimonthly life story writing group at Monroeville Public Library in the greater Pittsburgh area. She also has begun WE WRITE! Creative Writing University, currently hosted by Monroeville Public Library. She is frequently found teaching courses for the Osher Life Long Learning Programs at both the University of Pittsburgh and Carnegie Mellon University related to various aspects of writing. While Sharon can be a competent and high powered writer, leader and teacher, she is also one of the kindest people I know.

Fiery Italian Stir Fry

Sharon writes, "I discovered this dish by accident, and it's infinitely variable. The main thing that sets it apart from any number of classic Italian dishes is the inclusion of crushed red pepper flakes in the preparation. Whatever vegetables you have on hand will work, fresh or frozen, pasta shape is negotiable, and sauce is optional. Amounts of each ingredient depend on the number of people you are feeding. I like to vary the veggies to get color variety."

Ingredients:

Your choice of pasta (my favorite for this is penne. Mostaccioli, ziti, rigatoni, rotini or similar shapes work equally well.)

Mixture of your choice of sliced fresh or frozen vegetables — about 1 cup total per serving: onion wedges and sliced (Portobello) mushrooms go with everything, plus sliced sweet peppers of any and all colors, broccoli, cauliflower, thinly sliced carrots, or zucchini. Hot peppers such as banana peppers or jalapeños are great.

virgin olive oil for sautéing and dressing pasta

Italian herb mixture

finely minced garlic to taste

crushed red pepper flakes (omit if you use hot peppers)

parmesan cheese

Italian sausage cut into small chunks (optional)

Directions:
Cook pasta per package instructions. Set aside.

While pasta cooks, lightly sauté vegetables in olive oil in large skillet just to warm and soften. If you use sausage, cook it before adding vegetables. Sprinkle with herbs and red pepper. Set aside if done before pasta.

Combine pasta with vegetables, drizzle with oil, and sprinkle liberally with Parmesan cheese.

Variations:
Add small chunks of Italian sausage (mild or spicy) to stir-fry mix.

Add your favorite spaghetti sauce to pan just as veggies finish cooking. Simmer to warm.

Talk, Mime, and Words on Napkins: Xuerong/Sharon

Sharon/Xuerong was captivated by the beautiful scenery as she traveled the U.S. as a visiting research professor from Nanjing, China.

It was a beautiful, warm, sunny day in the fall of 2012. I had just updated my ID card for my Osher studies at the University of Pittsburgh and was enjoying the walk down Fifth Avenue past Hillman Library and back to my car to return home. Just then, a young Asian woman walked up to me with a sheet of paper in her hand. She looked professional, wearing a fashionable dress and scarf and sensible but attractive heels. She had a gentle smile on her face as she approached me and said something hard for me to understand, motioning to the paper. On the paper was written:

> *the School of Education, Posvar Hall, and the Quality Inn, Blvd. of the Allies.*

She was asking me if I could direct her to the Quality Inn.

Through some mime, some English, and some struggling for words, I communicated that the Quality Inn was too far to walk and that I would drive her. I showed her my Osher ID card, freshly printed and still in my hand, to attest to the fact that I was a Pitt student and safe to ride with in a car. We walked the several blocks to my car, struggling but managing to talk in English and Chinese. I know no Chinese, and she struggled with spoken English but actually did quite well, I thought.

While we were riding in my car, I learned that her name was Xuerong—she wrote it down in a book she had with her. I confirmed that she had just come from the School of Education at Pitt in Posvar Hall. She said she had an interview which, again, she wrote down. She was a visiting scholar from the university in Nanjing where she works as a researcher. She earned her PhD from the university in Shanghai in education. I told her I studied higher education at Pitt too.

We continued to mix mime, writing, and struggling with spoken English, but we managed to converse. Xuerong had her luggage in the motel. She still had to find a place to live. I wrote my name and phone number in Xuerong's book. Xuerong was very gracious and grateful that I had driven her to the Quality Inn. I dropped her off and wished her well—hoping that I would hear from her again. That is how we met.

Xuerong did call me on the phone. We struggled to converse briefly without paper and pencil to assist us. We had difficulty exchanging email addresses over the phone too. I thought she was saying "s" for "x" for her name in her email address. She got a new American acquaintance to get my email address and to give me hers. We began emailing and still send brief emails from time to time. Xuerong found an apartment on Forbes Avenue in Squirrel Hill where she rented from a woman. who is from the Philippines and was married to an American. Xuerong had her own quarters but shared the kitchen.

Xuerong and I met for coffee one week later. I drove us to Jitters Café, a coffeehouse that I frequent in Shadyside. Harry, a worker at Jitters whose mother is Korean, was very gracious in greeting Xuerong. Sitting outside Jitters on that warm, sunny October morning, we had a wonderful hour and a half visit. Our conversation was a combination of talk, mime, and writing words on napkins. We shared life stories, and I learned that she has a mother, father, two sisters, and a brother. Her parents live in Shanghai. She talked about how clean Pittsburgh was and how polluted some cities in China were. I pointed out that Pittsburgh was once polluted and more prosperous. Xuerong likes Pittsburgh. She mentioned that she may visit a friend in either Gainesville, Florida, or New York City over Christmas vacation. I assured her she would enjoy either. We also talked about cooking, and Xuerong pointed out that she likes cooking and eating vegetables.

Sitting in the warm sun, I delighted in talking with Xuerong. She told me she was writing a paper on higher education in China to fulfill her obligations to a school program in China. Then she would study American higher education here at Pitt. I found it interesting and fun to make this new acquaintance. Driving her back to Hillman Library at Pitt where she spent many hours studying, I told her we would have coffee again soon. I have invited her to coffee. I also had her over to my house for a dinner from time to time. I looked forward to developing this new friendship. By the way, Xuerong took the name Sharon as her American name.

I continued to have coffee with Sharon when I attended classes at Pitt. Also, since I told Martha, Dee, and Sandie about Sharon during one of our Oglebay retreats, they have adopted her too. We all had dinner at Sandie's house with Sharon. Sharon came to my house for pot roast with potatoes, carrots, and gravy. She remarked, "This is the best American food I ever ate." She took me to an authentic Chinese restaurant for dinner one evening. We had several dishes, but Sharon pointed out that the one with fishes was the most like her dinners at home. We continued to meet frequently for coffee and occasionally for dinner.

*Sharon and me enjoying her first American
hamburger and French fries at the Elbow Room*

Sadly for me, she returned to China in September, 2013. She was a delight, and I miss her gentle ways. We continue to email. She once wrote that she learned something important from me. She said, "I always thought work was a duty and a responsibility. You taught me that it should also be fun." I was honored by this response.

Mushroom and Broccoli Stir Fry

Sharon loves cooking vegetables, and, right now, eating broccoli is her favorite. Here is a recipe from Sharon which she has chosen to include here:

Ingredients:
fresh mushrooms
broccoli
1 red pepper
oyster sauce, to taste (about 1 T per 1 c. veggies)
salt, to taste
monosodium glutamate (optional)

Directions:
First, wash and cut mushrooms and broccoli into pieces, cut red pepper in strips

Second, put the oil into the hot pan. then put ginger, put mushroom, stir fry for a while, add broccoli and red pepper, stir fry quickly

Third, add salt, monosodium glutamate, oyster sauce

Yield: 1 serving

A Gentle Man: Keith

Keith inspires our writing group to write well, and he inspires me to be kind.

A kind and gentle man from my life story writing group in Monroeville Library, Keith is someone I have known for nearly three years. Keith's career was as a special education high school teacher. He had a significant influence on his students. He recounts a story of a student whom he encounters with his girlfriend. The student exclaims to his girlfriend, "This is the man who changed my life," as he embraced and acknowledged Keith.

He and his partner, Louise, make a Christmas cake to share with friends during the holidays. He gave one to me this year. It was delicious and shows how thoughtful Keith and Louise are. Once when I was experiencing some stress, they invited me over for some homemade soup for the soul. Also, helpful and kind, Keith offers to share materials with me as I take on the challenge of facilitating my own life story writing group.

Keith writes powerful stories with keen description. They are often about his days growing up on his family farm and usually include humorous aspects and twists to them. For example, Keith created a story about being in high school and driving through the town in the farm truck where he was sitting on a huge heap of hay. It never seemed to occur to anyone that this might be an enormously unsafe way to travel the roads and highways. What was more amazing was that nothing ever happened during this ride.

He also writes in the most lovingly way about his parents. He describes a caring, nurturing mother, who tirelessly does all of the cooking for the family. She plans delicious menus and prepares them, and she bakes delectable pies and cakes. What a feast his Sundays as a child were with people dropping over to enjoy the homemade cooking. His father lovingly expected his son to work hard on the farm but "not to grow up to be a farmer." It is never-ending, back – breaking work, all day, every day, 24-7.

Keith is a most caring and compassionate man. Yet he can always see the humor in situations. Adult development specialists state that adults who survive and thrive continue to initiate new friendships. My friendship with Keith is one of those new friendships for me.

Molasses Crinkles

Keith writes, "This cookie is similar to the one my mother made. I don't have her exact recipe, but they taste like the ones she had for us as an after school snack."

Ingredients:
¾ c. soft shortening
1 egg
¼ c. molasses
2 t baking soda
1 c. brown sugar, packed
¼ t salt
½ t cloves
1 t cinnamon
1 t ginger
2-¼ c. flour
granulated sugar for tops of cookies

Directions:
Mix shortening, sugar, egg, and molasses thoroughly. Blend all dry ingredients except granulated sugar. Stir wet mixture into dry mixture. Chill.

Preheat oven to 375 degrees. Roll dough into 1-inch balls. Dip tops in sugar.

Place balls, sugared side up, on greased baking sheet. Bake 7 to 8 minutes or until set, but not hard.

My Old, New Friend: Marsha

Marsha now

A letter came in the mail. It had been forwarded to me from Carlow University where I had worked until my retirement three years earlier. I was still listed as faculty because I worked with master's candidates on their thesis documents. The return address listed Marsha

Smith with another last name, a married name, tacked on. Could this be the Marsha Smith of my high school years?

I had thought of her from time to time but could not Google "Smith." I opened the envelope with great anticipation.

It was a beautifully crafted letter, which reminisced about volunteering with "an Ellen" to be school representatives for the Red Feather Community Chest (now United Way) in greater-Cleveland. Was I, she asked, the Ellen who, after attending together a representatives' gathering, had tried walking blocks and more blocks to get a ride home, only to shed our stylish high-heel shoes from our aching feet—to walk unstylishly in just our nylon stockings?

Marsha in high school

Marsha mentioned that, when she learned that the Parma Senior High School 50th Class Reunion committee could not locate me, she decided to try the Internet herself to search. That's how she came to write me. Was I—the Ellen of Carlow University–that Ellen? In her letter, she said she had found that I had published some professional writings and looked one up on the Internet. Yes, she had done her homework. I was indeed that Ellen.

How do you catch up on 50 years? Marsha started by telling me about her married life and home near Denver, how years of her career in magazine publishing were spent commuting to Chicago to resurrect a publishing company from near ruin to prosperity again. Now retired with her husband, she had brought her 97-year-old mother to live with them in their hillside home. I was so impressed. I was also so excited to be embarking on the reviving of a very old friendship from high school.

Marsha remembers her school years as facing the frigid morning in Parma, Ohio, with wintry walks to the school bus stop, carrying bagged lunches of tuna fish sandwiches, being embarrassed about her stomach making weird sounds, and having no dates... always wishing to be popular, longing to wear the couple of party dresses in her closet. My high school years had personally been very unhappy. Cleveland had been a sad place for me, so when I left, I never looked back. High school and adolescence could be difficult. Now I was ready to integrate those high school years back into my life, and Marsha was helping me do that, both of us reaching back to find fun times in the midst of whatever angst we had been feeling a half century before. I got to renew a wonderful friendship, as well.

I remember Marsha from high school as a petite young woman with curly red hair and impish smile. She was always warm, friendly, and kind—and she was very bright. She was an art major. We both were Thespians, in the Senior Class Play, as well as Honor Society members. In those days, we did not talk about our personal lives, so I had no idea what Marsha's high school journey was like—and she had no idea of mine. We just liked each other in the moment.

Now, we are reconnecting. We send frequent emails. At my request, she has sent some of her more recent projects—one a magazine for young children and their families about healthy eating, fresh-air play, and the fun of learning. I liked how the magazine accurately reflected what we know about child development. Another magazine for children was about airplanes and the science of flight, published with her pilot husband, for children attending an air show. The writing is outstanding, but the graphics are incredible. She is so talented. Then I shared with her some of my life story writings, to which she responded with sensitivity.

Of course, she and I do age-appropriate moaning and groaning about our bodies growing old—too many aches and pains to count. We are developmentally on target with the moaning. Marsha wonders whether we ruined our bodies by walking in stocking feet down dirty city sidewalks years ago. I am delighted to have Marsha's friendship in my life again. I am so appreciative that she initiated this renewal.

Having sent me a recent picture of herself, I can still see shadows of the curly red hair and the impish smile. It evokes all the love and care I felt for her in high school.

Marsha's Saturday Morning Scones

Ingredients:

½ c. raisins, simmered in 1 tbsp. Amaretto and a splash of water (may substitute raisins with dried cranberries or chopped dates)

1 beaten egg

¼ c. milk

¼ c. heavy cream

1/3 c. white granulated sugar

2 c. flour

2 t baking powder

½ t baking soda

1 t salt

5-½ T cold unsalted butter, cut into pieces

½ c. chopped pecans

cinnamon

brown sugar, raw, or turbinado sugar, if desired

Directions:

Preheat oven to 400 degrees.

Cover an ungreased cookie sheet with parchment paper.

In large mixing bowl, combine dry ingredients. Set aside.

In medium mixing bowl, beat egg. Add milk and cream, then sugar. Mix until creamy. Set aside.

Cut butter into dry ingredients with a pastry cutter until mixture resembles crumbs.

Using large spatula, add creamy mixture to dry ingredients. Add nuts and raisins. Mix until dough "comes together." If it seems too sticky to work with, add a tablespoon of flour.

With floured hands, gather and turn out dough onto a floured cutting board. Flatten dough into a 10" circle. Generously sprinkle brown sugar to cover the dough. Repeat with cinnamon.

Lift one edge of the dough and roll inward until all dough is in the shape of a roll.

Fold roll in half, bringing ends together, then in half again, forming a ball shape. Press down into a 10" circle once again. The brown sugar and cinnamon will be streaked through the dough. Brush top of dough with heavy cream and sprinkle with raw or brown sugar.

Cut the circle into 8 pieces as you would a pie.

Place wedges an inch apart on the parchment paper-covered cookie sheet.

Bake for 17-20 minutes or until golden.

Serve warm from the oven with condiments. The scones are extra delicious when spread with a mixture of lemon yogurt and sour cream.

Across the Aisle Partners and Soul Mates: Veronica

Veronica and I encourage each other to write and to publish and are a fine audience for each other's writings.

When I was in tenth grade English class, Mr. Mayer assigned us, "Write your own creative story and bring the draft to class in one week." I wrote a story about a five-year-old little girl, who carried her doll with her everywhere. One day, she misplaced—thought she had lost—her doll. She was heartbroken. For several days, she sadly looked for her doll and could not find it. Then one day, unexpectedly, when she went to reach for a cookie in the cookie jar, she found her doll there—inside the cookie jar. She was so happy to be reunited with her doll.

I brought the draft of my story to class as I was directed to do. My classmate, Veronica, then called Ronnie, sat across the aisle from me. We had become friends over the time of the class—it was now in the spring of the school year. We talked before and after class and, when we could, sometimes even during class. In class, Mr. Mayer directed, "Exchange papers with the person across the aisle to get some suggestions for improvement." I entrusted my story to Veronica. She read it and made the comment, "Your story is lovely, but don't you think it would be a stronger story if she found her doll and discovered that she no longer needed it as she had in the past?"

Of course, Veronica was right, but it did not meet my psychological need to reconnect with lost loved ones. I rewrote the story anyway—it was a much more mature ending. I got an "A" on the story thanks to Veronica's wise and sensitive guidance. This interaction was so powerful to me that the memory has stuck with me to this day. It was difficult for me to change that story; it was in my soul. I really wanted to write it my way. However, I felt that Veronica was right about it being a stronger ending with the little girl no longer needing her doll. Now, I am aware that this story met my psychological need to deal with the early childhood theme of loss and reconnection. Then, I only knew that this was the story that was inside of me.

I went to my 50th high school class reunion, and I was disappointed that Veronica was not present. After I received my Memory Book, with classmates' addresses, phone numbers, and email information, I immediately examined it to see if Veronica was listed. She not only allowed this information to be included, but wrote a brief description of her life as each graduate was invited to do. One aspect she highlighted was being a former newspaper and magazine writer and now a ghostwriter. Was her career choice foreshadowed in her helpful guidance in rewriting the ending of my story so many years earlier? I was delighted to see her write up and wanted to reconnect with this most interesting person. So I sent her an email, and we have been emailing ever since. "It is like we are sitting across the aisle in English class only better," she wrote to me.

We write meaningful volumes to each other every few days. It has only been a month and a half, but it feels like we have been in touch for years. We really resonate with each other. We share a personal writing with each other attached to every email. Her essays are poetry, filled with metaphors and poignant insights. They are often related to nature, tied to the natural as well as spiritual, and demonstrate her Buddhist orientation to life. In her writing, "Snow Melts," Veronica describes a horse's body's warmth melting the snow around it, just as personal "warmth" can diminish the "coldness" of humans nearby.

We have a number of things in common. We both have developed important, lasting relationships with many women. Like mine, her women friends are kind, caring, generous, and encouraging—and fun to be with. Both of us had families in high school that did not permit us to invite friends home, but we simply didn't know that about each other at that time. Obviously, we both love to write. On a more mundane level, we both got kicked out of a class for talking in high school. I almost ran into her at St. Francis de Sales Grade School when I transferred in seventh grade, but the Diocese of Cleveland changed the neighborhood she lived in so she attended a newly built school. I almost went to Bowling Green State University where she attended college, but I received a scholarship to Duquesne University at the last minute.

At this time, Veronica encourages me, "You should write a book," but adds, "if you want to do it." She generously offers to assist me as I take the next step, "I would be willing to edit it." Veronica is positive, caring, and compassionate. When I emailed her a story about my mother and, ultimately, the house my mother provided for me, Veronica responded. "Although the ending is bittersweet, it is a true love story. . . . And in the end, she did what every mother sets out to do—she gave birth to children who give love and care to everyone around them."

I am delighted to rekindle this friendship from many years past. I just love having her as my "pen pal" as she has pointed out. We are of the generation that talks about pen pals.

Maybe it is mature to be reunited with your treasured doll after all.

Sweet Potatoes á là Debbi

Veronica writes, "My friend Debbi Landis, who gave me this recipe, lived in a storybook Century House in New London, Ohio. She loved music, food and writing, and was a very special person."

Ingredients:
3 medium sweet potatoes, peeled and diced
1 medium red pepper, sliced or chopped
1 large onion, sliced
6 T olive oil
3 T tamari sauce

Directions:
Preheat oven to 425 degrees.

Combine vegetables in a large bowl. In a small bowl, mix oil and tamari. Add to vegetables and toss. Oil two 13x9 pans (don't use spray). Spread the vegetables on the pans in a single layer on each. Bake 15 minutes. Toss. Bake 10 to 15 minutes more, until browned. Serve warm or chilled—great both ways.

A Darwinian Walk: Joanne

Joanne captures the soul of a health educator and a scientist—and causes me to stretch.

She had her first pedicure at 68 years old, and she has a pumpkin painted on each of her big toe nails. Yes, she is playful.

Juxtaposed with this playfulness is a serious-minded and dedicated health educator, who did data collection through interviews about mental health and needed services in a community. In addition, she worked with the Student Health Center at the University of Florida, Gainesville, assisting students with AIDS. She also wrote curriculum for teaching college students at the University about the use of contraception. She accomplished all of this in the 70s, 80s, and 90s when these were trend-setting activities.

This is my friend, Joanne.

I knew her from Parma Senior High School. We had been in National Honor Society together. Joanne and I had participated in a wonderful, innovative course, Arts Seminar, together. In this class, three instructors from literature, music, and art team-taught an integration of the arts. Weren't we fortunate? We even studied and attended a performance of *Madame Butterfly* in downtown Cleveland—an unheard of classroom activity in 1963. We also shared Miss Givens, a sweet but exacting senior English teacher, who geared us up for college as she scared the bejeebers out of us by using blue books for our final exam.

Joanne and I had lost touch with each other over the 50 years from graduation to the PSH 50th year reunion. When I received my Memory Book from the reunion, I found a picture of Joanne in high school looking just as I remembered her. The Memory Book also contained her present contact information in Gainesville, Florida. Until then, the only person I had known in Gainesville was my sister. It was fortuitous that I learn about Joanne's also being in Gainesville. I emailed Joanne and asked her what she was doing in Gainesville—and, as they say, the rest is history.

We have been emailing ever since, and I am delighted to rekindle this friendship.

I unexpectedly returned to Gainesville twice during 2013—for a vacation and for my sister's retirement party. Ordinarily, my sister and I alternate yearly visits to each other's homes. I had just been to her city in August. But the retirement party called me back in September. Joanne had invited me to get together for lunch, and I had happily agreed. We met at a mom and pop restaurant called Civilization near her home. Afterward, we sat outside and relished a delicious, vegetarian-type lunch—although I added some chicken to the mix in my lovely vegetarian burrito. We sprinkled conversation about PSH memories with talk of technology, books, outdoor activities, and so on. There was no lack of conversation. We were comfortable with each other. Afterward, we went to her house where I went for a lovely walk in her gardens in the peaceful, pensive style of Darwin, who used his walks to clarify his thoughts. I also enjoyed a visit in her charming home with her interesting, kind husband, David. Joanne and David met through their local Sierra Club, a grassroots effort to change the nation's attitudes about land conservation, personal responsibility in using natural resources, and education about the environment. What a fine combination! Joanne can be playful and mindful of life's responsibilities. What a fun afternoon! Joanne and I made a commitment to continue to keep in touch, and we continue through our frequent emails.

Beef Oriental

Joanne shares a recipe handed down from her mother, who "probably adapted it from a newspaper recipe."

Ingredients:

1 lb. ground beef, browned with onions and drained
1 large sweet onion, chopped
1 c. celery, chopped
1 can bean sprouts, drained, or the equivalent fresh
    sprouts
1 14-oz. can condensed mushroom soup
1 c. water
¼ c. soy sauce
½ c. rice, uncooked
Optional: toasted almonds silvers or dry roasted peanuts to sprinkle on top after baking

Directions:

Stir all ingredients together and spread in an 8" or 9" Pyrex™ square dish.

Bake one and a half hours at 350 degrees.

Persistence: Barb

I had been trying to reach Barb for two months, leaving her frequent voice mail messages. She was someone I knew in high school. I had earlier renewed my friendship with Marsha. When Marsha could not go to the 50th class reunion, I hoped to see another cherished high school friend, Barb. I was really looking forward to seeing Barb there. I had such fond memories of her in high school. I finally decided to be daring go to the reunion alone—someone would surely invite me to sit with them at their table. As life would have it, the day I sent in my check to make the reunion payment, I reached Barb by phone.

It was wonderful to talk with Barb on the phone. She is the warm and caring person that I knew in high school. She told me about her five grown children. I described my career and personal life. She even owns a women's football team that won all of their games this year. We talked about volunteering, and she mentioned her work on the school board for 10 years. She also talked about the past seven years which she has spent volunteering at Parma Hospital under the guidance of the volunteer director, Mr. Jim Mayer, our former drama teacher and English teacher. We had fun just reminiscing about him and the plays.

Barb was a very talented actor in high school. I had the good fortune of being in drama classes with her, and we would pair up to do excerpts from plays. Once she played Queen Elizabeth I, and I was Mary,

Queen of Scots. It was so much fun to work with her because she was so expressive and it would bring out the best in me. Barb had the important roles in the junior class and senior class plays and in the plays for state competition. She won the Thespian Club award for best actor her senior year in high school.

When I drove to meet Barb in Parma for the reunion, it was with some anxiety. Would we connect as we had in high school? Amazingly, we did. We met for a light lunch at Panera's—she picked me up from the hotel. It was comfortable being with her. She is kind and generous, and it showed from the onset of our visit. We parted to ready ourselves for the reunion. She and her husband, Loree, picked me up. He too was kind, generous, and polite. I most enjoyed talking with Barb for she is easy to talk with. She introduced me to Mr. and Mrs. Mayer from high school drama. I had a fine conversation with both about their current endeavors. Mr. Mayer teaches 10-week training sessions yearly to the spiritual volunteers in Parma Hospital, and, for fun, does the cooking for him and his wife. Mrs. Mayer still does acting gigs and is currently playing Mary Todd Lincoln. I also got to thank Mr. Mayer in person for all the kindnesses he showed to me in high school. Meeting Barb and Mr. and Mrs. Mayer again made the reunion totally worthwhile.

The next morning, Barb and I went out for a long breakfast before I drove back to Pittsburgh. We talked easily and continued to catch up on the many years that had passed. She showed me loving pictures of her family who look like they have fun together. We parted with words to continue this renewed friendship.

Strawberry Cream Pretzel Dessert

Barb has included this elegant dessert served for special occasions.

Crust:
Ingredients:
2 c. crushed pretzels
1/3 c. sugar
½ c. melted butter

Directions:
Preheat oven to 325 degrees. Mix these 3 ingredients. Spread into a 9 x 13 pan. Bake for 8 minutes.

Filling:
Ingredients:
1 large cream cheese
½ c. sugar
1 8-oz. Cool Whip

Directions:
With beater, add these 3 in order and whip. Set aside.

Topping:
Ingredients:
1 8-svg. pkg. strawberry gelatin
2 c. boiling water
2 10-oz. pkgs. frozen strawberries

Directions:

Combine ingredients. Chill until a jelly consistency.

Cool crust. Add beaten filling over crust. Top with partially set gelatin mixture. Chill until firm.

Serve in squares and enjoy.

APÉRITIF

Enjoying the after dinner drink with dessert as the day is winding down.

Life is good: Me

Me at Jitters Café, Christmas 2013

I savor the delightful taste of St. Germain, a liqueur from Paris, France. Made of "hand selected" elder flowers, the flowers of elderberries, and citrus and tropical fruits, this liqueur was introduced to me by my friends, Rosemarie and Janice D. This drink accompanies a wonderful piece of carrot cake, a delicious treat. I cut a small piece and savor its delicate taste. I am seeking to show the restraint that I value as I enter this phase of my life at 68 years. My friends have nourished me well over the years. I am satiated. I am ready to eat-in-moderation. I am full and now can do that, thanks to my friends. I would like to think that, in the process of life, I have fed my friends too, that in the long-of-life, things balance out and become reciprocal. I hope so. I believe it is so.

Carrot Cake

As a result of a conversation with Dr. Hazlett about carrot cake, she suggested this recipe. I tried it, and it was so superb that I've baked it again and again for various celebratory occasions and regular days as a special treat.

Ingredients:
1 c. all-purpose flour, sifted
1/2 t baking soda
1/2 t baking powder
3/4 t cinnamon
1 c. white sugar
3/4 c. vegetable oil
2 eggs
1-1/2 c. carrots, finely grated

Directions:
Preheat oven to 350 degrees.

Grease a 9x9-inch pan.

Sift flour into a large bowl. Add baking soda, baking powder, and cinnamon. Set aside.

In a large mixing bowl, combine sugar and oil. Add eggs, one at a time, and beat well with each added egg. Gradually add dry ingredients, beating until just combined. Gently fold in grated carrots. Pour into pan.

Bake 35-40 minutes or until toothpick comes out clean.

Icing:
Ingredients:
¼ c. butter, softened
1 8-oz. package of cream cheese, softened
3 c. powdered sugar
2 t vanilla

Directions:
Using mixer, cream butter and cream cheese together.
Gradually add powdered sugar. Add vanilla, stirring just
enough to blend.

Adapted from McManus, Carol. *Table Talk: Food,
Family, Love.* Edgartown, MA: Vineyard Stories, 2008, p.
87.

List of Abbreviations

'	foot
"	inch
c.	cup
lb.	pound
oz.	ounce
pkg .	package
svg.	serving
t	teaspoon
T	tablespoon

31869348R00211

Made in the USA
Charleston, SC
31 July 2014